Please return or renew this item
by the last date shown. You may
return items to any East Sussex
Library. You may renew books
by telephone or the internet.

East Sussex
County Council

0345 60 80 195 for renewals
0345 60 80 196 for enquiries

Library and Information Services
eastsussex.gov.uk/libraries

'This book clearly describes a technique that can be employed to very good effect in a range of therapies. I recommend its use.'
Windy Dryden PhD, Professor of Psychotherapeutic Studies, Goldsmiths, University of London

'PBT is a very simple yet powerful form of therapy. It has the potential to change lives for the better and in doing so have a positive impact on the stresses in today's world.'
Lynn Crilly, author and counsellor

'This approach makes sense to everyone, from teachers to psychologists to parents and students. It is wonderfully simple, but simply effective. I am finding it to be a great tool for my work.'
Stelios N. Georgiou, Professor of Educational Psychology, University of Cyprus

'The Shirrans have synthesized elements of CBT, NLP and hypnotherapy to create a brilliantly simple and powerful technique for making life choices and effecting positive change.'
Dr Leila Edwards, Principal, Transformations Institute

'The PBT concept addresses the vital moment of decision-making in all our lives: continue with the old pattern, or break it and create a new one. It is an effective and modern approach to an age-old problem. As the book says, "all the best ideas are simple ones."'
Nick Clements, author of *The New Ages of Men*

PAUSE BUTTON THERAPY®

• PAUSE • THINK • DECIDE • ACT

MARTIN AND MARION SHIRRAN
WITH FIONA GRAHAM

HAY HOUSE

Australia • Canada • Hong Kong • India
South Africa • United Kingdom • United States

First published and distributed in the United Kingdom by:
Hay House UK Ltd, 292B Kensal Rd, London W10 5BE.
Tel.: (44) 20 8962 1230; Fax: (44) 20 8962 1239.
www.hayhouse.co.uk

Published and distributed in the United States of America by:
Hay House, Inc., PO Box 5100, Carlsbad, CA 92018-5100.
Tel.: (1) 760 431 7695 or (800) 654 5126;
Fax: (1) 760 431 6948 or (800) 650 5115.
www.hayhouse.com

Published and distributed in Australia by:
Hay House Australia Ltd, 18/36 Ralph St, Alexandria NSW 2015.
Tel.: (61) 2 9669 4299; Fax: (61) 2 9669 4144.
www.hayhouse.com.au

Published and distributed in the Republic of South Africa by:
Hay House SA (Pty), Ltd, PO Box 990, Witkoppen 2068.
Tel./Fax: (27) 11 467 8904. www.hayhouse.co.za

Published and distributed in India by:
Hay House Publishers India, Muskaan Complex, Plot No.3, B-2,
Vasant Kunj, New Delhi – 110 070. Tel.: (91) 11 4176 1620;
Fax: (91) 11 4176 1630.
www.hayhouse.co.in

Distributed in Canada by:
Raincoast, 9050 Shaughnessy St, Vancouver, BC V6P 6E5.
Tel.: (1) 604 323 7100; Fax: (1) 604 323 2600

Text © Martin Shirran, Marion Shirran and Fiona Graham, 2012

The moral rights of the authors have been asserted.

The information given in this book should not be treated as a substitute for professional medical advice; always consult a medical practitioner. Any use of information in this book is at the reader's discretion and risk. Neither the authors nor the publisher can be held responsible for any loss, claim or damage arising out of the use, or misuse, of the suggestions made, the failure to take medical advice, or for any material on third party websites.

A catalogue record for this book is available from the British Library.

ISBN: 978-1-78180-048-5

Printed and bound in Great Britain by TJ International, Padstow, Cornwall.

CONTENTS

AKNOWLEDGEMENTS

Firstly, we must thank the hundreds of clients and volunteers who visited our clinic in Spain. Without them, and the thousands of hours of one-to-one therapy time that was accumulated, this book would never have been written.

Thanks also to both Gay Jones and Dr Theano Kalavana for their inspiring and professional contributions – their knowledge and experience in the field of Psychology proved invaluable.

The initial trials regarding the use of Pause Button Therapy with children were undertaken at the wonderful Twickenham Primary School in Kingstanding, Birmingham. Our thanks go to the excellent staff, pupils and parents, and special thanks to our friend and deputy head, John Taylor.

During the early trials of PBT we met a brilliant young therapist called Gemma Keep. Her interest and excitement were often contagious. We have included some of her suggestions in the book.

A special thank you to our dear friend Jon Ashby of Vector Productions, not only for putting the Pause Button Therapy website together but also for filming the school children who trialled PBT, and other case studies. Thanks for helping us out so many times over the years with all matters technical.

It is no secret that the book would never have seen the light of day had it not been for the hundreds of hours of hard work, and patience, of our co-author, Fiona Graham. We hope all those endless hours spent in front of the computer, the sleepless nights and hundreds of miles driven up and down the coast roads of Spain all now seem worthwhile.

Finally, we must thank the team at Hay House, especially Carolyn Thorne and our editor, Barbara Vesey. This is our first project with a professional publishing house: we were, we are sure, sometimes a little naïve. Thanks for your patience.

Martin and Marion Shirran

INTRODUCTION

This is a book for anyone who's ever made a mistake in their life, and never wants to make one again. It's for anyone – *anyone* – who wants to make a change.

Pause Button Therapy® – PBT – is a new therapy based on an idea so simple a small child can understand it. In UK primary school trials, children proved they were not only able to grasp the concept, but to incorporate it positively into their lives after just a few hours' tuition. Yet PBT also shows beneficial results when used to help treat a wide range of behavioural issues, from road rage to relationship problems, and from OCD to bulimia. PBT has also been used successfully to treat obesity and addictions. A number of public and commercial applications have also been identified.

PBT uses the idea of the Pause, Rewind, Fast Forward and Play buttons on remote control devices to help people give themselves more thinking time when faced with decisions. It teaches them how to ensure they make the best possible use of that time to weigh up the potential consequences of their actions. This allows them to incorporate a blend of CBT (Cognitive Behaviour Therapy) with PBT to live more successfully in the present.

Martin and Marion Shirran not only promise – they deliver. PBT – developed, tried and tested over the past three years – is reaching a wider market already heralded by other therapists, and has been trialled with existing clients in both Europe and the US.

Critically, in an era of ever-increasing behavioural problems in young adults, we are also planning to run trials in Young Offender Institutions.

We have been fortunate enough to attract interest in the potential of PBT from educational experts and therapists alike. Two of them have contributed chapters to illustrate their belief in the sound psychological and behavioural basis for PBT, and to bring to a wider audience some of the trials already undertaken in schools.

Involved in education since the mid-1980s, former teacher Gay Jones, MA, BEd (Hons) has specialized in school improvement and change for over 20 years.

In 2011, Gay developed PBT for use with children and young people in schools and other settings. She has created support materials and training sessions for teaching and support staff, children and parents.

Gay's chapter (Chapter 10) explains the processes that underlie PBT. Understanding how brain development and psychology influence the use of PBT with young people is a key skill for teachers, parents and other childcare workers. She describes how to present PBT to children and young people for daily use.

Dr Theano V. Kalavana has a PhD in Health Psychology, a BSc in Philosophy, Education and Psychology with Specialization in Psychology, and an MSc in Health Psychology.

Her main area of research focuses on the contribution of self-regulation cognitions and skills in altering health behaviours. She has undertaken further training in the US in self-regulation and health. She has taught as a visiting lecturer at two major institutions in Cyprus and some of her projects have received EU funding. Dr Kalavana has spoken at a number of international professional conferences and has published her research in various scientific journals.

She has written that she believes it is likely that PBT is the only tool in existence right now that bridges the gap between behavioural intention and actual behaviour, making it an effective therapeutic procedure leading to successful behaviour change.

The Pause Button technique was developed out of the Shirrans' work within their own weight-loss therapy, Gastric *mind* Band. They found clients struggled with facing their various triggers and behaviours, and this led to the overeating which had made them overweight.

They achieved the best results by encouraging the clients not only to 'stop and think' when facing their 'demon foods', but also training them to visualize, feel, experience and ultimately think through the potential consequences of their actions.

The sideways development into other behaviour interventions came after an anger management client asked about one of the PBT devices he'd spotted at the Shirrans' clinic in Spain. Martin suggested he trialled the device, and this proved that the PBT visualization technique was likely to be just as vivid and just as successful with many other behaviours. So far, nothing has really proved out of range.

We were gratified and encouraged when academics such as Gay Jones and Theano Kalavana came on board, convinced there were cast iron, scientifically credible explanations for the success of PBT. And that confidence has proved right.

We now realize there is a large body of research surrounding the theories of Time Perspective made widely known by Professor Philip Zimbardo, i.e., the way in which a person's attitude to the importance of, or prioritization of, the past, present and future can colour their everyday actions. Far more difficult to write than understand, this theory encompasses the idea that people who floss regularly, for example, think ahead to how long their teeth might need to last. They are future thinkers. Students who would rather leave writing a dissertation until the last few days before submission are present thinkers. People constantly looking to what might have happened in previous times are past thinkers.

To put PBT to best use, you need to grasp the principle that you can begin to choose what will happen in the future, if you understand how important the shape of that future is to you.

The scope of PBT is almost limitless. Schools – we know its success already. Prisons/Young Offender Institutions – who wouldn't like to reduce re-offending rates by any per cent if only we could help criminals see the full effect of their actions on their life? In healthcare: might the overweight think twice if they knew the side effects of obesity? Would youngsters take more care choosing shoes if they thought about how crippling foot problems can be? And those are just a few examples.

In commerce too – in-flight cabin crew are known to have to deal with all manner of problems. Maybe on occasion the

Pause Button would help defuse an awkward 'situation'? Would customer service staff benefit from another technique to see them through a provocative day's calls?

Does anyone in your family have issues with road rage? Alcohol dependency? Panic attacks? Anger management? By now you should be seeing just how PBT offers a helping hand (well, button at least!) for so many problem areas in life. Maybe it can help you too.

Pause. Think. Decide. Act.

GLOSSARY OF THERAPIES

You will see a number of therapies mentioned in this book.

CBT (Cognitive Behaviour Therapy) asks the individual to challenge the way their thoughts can be inaccurate – *thoughts* as opposed to *facts*. Once they recognize these 'sabotaging' thoughts, they can begin to overcome them.

NLP (Neuro Linguistic Programming) enables people to change their experience of reality by changing how they represent it to themselves. By understanding and working with the way language affects the subconscious, and techniques that reorganize the underlying sensory data in the mind, NLP empowers people to make the changes they desire. Incorporating creative visualization, it enables the widening of beliefs so you can 'see yourself' in another, different, better state of mind, with all the changes that accompany your new self-image. Focusing on this new 'blueprint' enables your subconscious mind to create a new set of responses and behaviours.

Guided Imagery is a technique in which the client is encouraged to see into the future by taking them through alternative scenarios in their mind's eye.

Hypnotherapy works because any suggestions made while the subconscious mind is receptive during deep relaxation are far more likely to be 'accepted'; the subconscious is more influential on our behaviour than the conscious mind, so in day-to-day life the suggestions can begin to take effect without any conscious effort.

Life Architecture is the name we've given to a combination of various therapies, each being used to underpin the other.

Pause Button Therapy®, the subject of this book, is the name given to the method of allowing people to freeze time and fast forward to see the consequences of their actions.

Gastric *mind* Band® (**GmB**), the subject of the Shirrans' first book, is a common-sense method of weight loss culminating in the 'virtual implantation' of a gastric band. All the above therapies are utilized within the technique.

In this book you'll also see references to Elite Clinics. This is the clinic in Spain owned and operated by the founders of the PBT and GmB therapies, Martin and Marion Shirran, and where they offer these and a variety of other therapies.

You can find further information about therapies available at the Elite Clinics by visiting www.eliteclinics.com

Pause Button Therapy International provides accredited training and support for employees, practitioners, schools, education services, youth offending teams, health professionals, local authorities, Primary Care Trusts and GP consortia. They also host a range of web-based resources and forums for both users and practitioners. Visit www.pausebuttontherapy.com

Further details of training courses can be found on pages 265–67.

None of the authors is medically trained in any way, though they are qualified in their own fields. PBT can be of great help with many disorders and conditions; however, where necessary, readers are also advised to seek medical advice.

In the text of the book we have intentionally mixed up the use of gender and person to help emphasize the fact that all the examples we talk about can refer equally to men, women, you, me, us, and so on. We're talking to, and about, anyone and everyone!

HOW THIS BOOK CAN HELP

A(not exhaustive) list of the problems, disorders and behaviours that could be helped by PBT:

Addictions

- Alcohol
- Cannabis
- Cocaine
- Heroin
- Nicotine

Behaviours and Choices

- Aggression
- Alcohol
- Anger management
- Anorexia
- Anxiety
- Avoiding making hasty phone calls
- Avoiding sending ill-judged texts, emails, instant messaging

- Bulimia
- Bullying
- Catastrophic thoughts
- Cocaine/Heroin/Cannabis
- Debt
- Depression
- Disciplining children
- Domestic violence
- Drink-driving
- Extreme risk-taking
- Gambling
- Impulse buying
- Lies/deception
- Medication abuse
- OCD
- Overeating
- Panic attacks
- Putting a stop to bullying (treating the bullies)
- Relationship issues
- Road rage
- Self-harm
- Smoking
- Teaching children self-control
- Texting/instant messaging
- Truancy
- Unwanted pregnancy

Commercial Uses

- Cabin crew

- Customer Service Staff

- Police officers

- Politicians

- Sales personnel

We feel PBT is equally applicable for use as a self-help tool OR in conjunction with residential, post-residential or non-residential therapy involving therapists working alongside the client.

PART 1

INTRODUCING PBT

ALL THE BEST IDEAS
ARE SIMPLE ONES

'Anything simple always interests me.'
DAVID HOCKNEY

How many times have you picked up a book and the opening line has read something like, 'This book will change your life'? Probably several times. You pick up the book, eagerly reading it through and waiting to get to the last page for the 'Miracle' to happen or for the 'Secret' to be revealed.

Well, this book is about something new, refreshing and, moreover, simple. It's something that has already changed people's lives for the better. And you won't have to read to the final chapter to realize how you can incorporate it into your life and benefit from its positive effect.

We're guessing that, if you've got as far as not only picking up but starting to read this book, the chances are you're not one of those improbably lucky, happy, healthy individuals, blissfully fulfilled in every detail of their lives – the ones who want for absolutely nothing and have absolutely zero regrets! Are we right? Well then, without further ado, we'd ask you to consider this: Might your life have taken a different course if, once or twice along the way, possibly several or loads of times – possibly even daily, and maybe even already today – you'd just stopped for a moment to actually think before making a choice? Taken a breath and considered the snap decision you were about to leap into, or the comment you were about to make?

Might you have achieved better grades in school? Not got into so much trouble with your parents? Married someone different? Managed to ditch that troublesome alcohol or nicotine addiction long ago?

Most probably all of those. It only takes a moment to make all the difference in life: maybe a couple of minutes, maybe just seconds, to reflect on whether you're on the right path or could be so much more confident, happier and healthier if you just thought things through that bit more carefully and decided that the outcome would be better all round if you took a different route.

Wouldn't it be brilliant if you got a second chance to make choices? What wouldn't we all give to rewind and take another shot at this, that or the other ill-judged action, the hastily sent text, or whatever our most recent slip-up was? Unfortunately, second chances rarely exist, and we know full well that, for most of us, making the right choice isn't always a piece of cake – in fact, our 'snap judgements' rarely turn out to be our best ones.

How does the song go? 'Regrets, I've had a few…' How many political leaders wish they had thought for a moment before they said what they said in a live TV interview? How many celebrities wish they could roll back the clock and not have been caught in such a compromising position by the paparazzi; and how many people in the world wish they could wind back time and not have that last drink which took them over the limit?

This is where our new, deceptively simple therapy comes in. We're not offering the impossible, just suggesting something you probably do most days anyway: Hit the Pause Button!

It's such a simple concept it almost beggars belief that no one has put together a therapy quite like this before. How many people don't know how to operate a remote control device? How many primary school children don't grasp the idea of Pause, Fast Forward, Rewind and Play? The basics are all there.

Pause Button Therapy (PBT) uses the idea of these remote control buttons to help you gain more thinking time when faced with decisions. It can teach you how to ensure you make the best possible use of that time to weigh up the potential consequences of your actions.

To break down the concept, let's say there's something happening in your life that you're finding stressful, or difficult, or annoying, or frightening, or appealing, or... it could be one of so very many emotions.

Emotions usually develop after some kind of stimulus, and progress to become motivation(s) if they are strong enough to make us act on the emotion – mentally, verbally or physically.

Your emotions can affect just you, or you and those around you. Buddhists place more importance on the effect on the individual, though the Western view is that an emotion is good or bad depending on how it affects the people around us or society as a whole.

How you react or respond to an emotion could make a huge impact on you and those around you. So, just imagine if you had a remote control for your mind. What would you do if you wanted to stop a DVD for a moment? Yes, press Pause. If you wanted to see the next scene of the film? Yes, Fast Forward. Go back to where you were and then view a different scene? Rewind and Fast Forward again. Go back to where you started and choose which scene/outcome you'd prefer to watch? That's right – Rewind and Play.

So, just for a moment, let's consider two words used in the last paragraph: *respond* and *react.* Do they mean the same thing? Not if you ponder this: wouldn't it be better to respond reflectively than react reflexively?

So what if you applied this, and the rest of the PBT armoury, to your stressful moments? Initially it may seem unlikely it would have made any difference to your exam results, or your relationship with your parents, or with alcohol, or bad temper – until you actually analyze what this could mean in real terms, in your own life.

You've wanted to cut out cigarettes for what seems like forever. Someone offers you one from their pack and, instead of reaching to take it gratefully, you press your thumb on your imaginary Pause Button; just visualize how it feels SO like a remote control.

Now you have the time, all the time you want to allow yourself, to think about what the choice might mean – what are the consequences of smoking? What are the consequences that most apply to you? Some people say it's health, some money, some the smell; for others it's the receding gums… for everyone it might be different. Which consequences mean the most to you? Which would motivate *you*?

Of course your problem may be something completely different, such as anger management, anxiety or Obsessive Compulsive Disorder (OCD). Whether your issue is something as basic as road rage (do I *really* want to tailgate the driver in front, endangering my toddler in the back seat, or shall I make the safer choice, giving myself thinking time by pressing Pause?). Or maybe it's something as potentially life-changing as being unfaithful to your partner. In each of these scenarios, taking the time to visualize the consequences, and see what means the most to you, can make all the difference, helping you to finally gain control.

Up until now, how much time have you actually spent considering the consequences of what you're about to say or do, and really thought about the potential effect your behaviour could have, not only on your own life, but also on those of your family, friends and other people, too?

Most people don't believe they have the ability to take that critical step to stop and think. They don't believe they can take control. By visualizing and actually physically going through the motions of pressing Pause, the mental block of 'how do I do this?' is removed.

> 'Everybody, sooner or later, sits down to a
> banquet of consequences.'
> **ROBERT LOUIS STEVENSON**

The concept of 'stop, think, act' has been used before; there's nothing new in it. What's different about PBT is that it encourages people to visualize, imagine, really mentally live out the consequences of their actions. It's much deeper than just pausing for a few seconds. It's about seeing how different decisions can play out in your life, your friends' lives and your family's lives. That's why the technique is so much more powerful and effective than just stopping and thinking.

People involved in PBT trials in UK schools have reported how empowering it was to gain control of their behaviour, sometimes for the first time. It proved to be a big boost to their self-esteem and confidence. Adults and children alike have found the technique simple and easy to incorporate into their day-to-day lives.

Later we'll look in much greater detail at how you can put the PBT tool to use in your own life. Right now, though, let's take a look at how the idea first came about.

The Development of PBT

PBT developed out of an initially trial, ultimately key, element of our weight-loss therapy, Gastric *mind* Band (G*m*B). Clients receive in-depth help with understanding their own flawed relationship with food and how to change it. The system includes elements of CBT, NLP, Hypnotherapy and Guided Imagery, which, when used to underpin each other, become the methodology we called 'Life Architecture'.

Many, if not all, people can be perfectly controlled and self-disciplined in some areas of their lives, yet struggle helplessly to control their behaviour with one specific thing. In the case of G*m*B clients, this was food.

In CBT terms, this struggle is known as Low Frustration Tolerance. It manifests as if the trigger factor, whatever it may be – fiery temper, speaking without thinking, for example – has an uncontrollable hold over the person. There seems to be no way to overcome that feeling; in the case of some things you consume, such as alcohol, cigarettes, food or drugs, in extreme cases it may make you feel the urge is so strong that if you don't give in you're convinced you'll die… at least that's what you'd be thinking at the time.

We needed a way to deal with this overwhelming, yet illogical, belief. Marion knew she'd read something in Judith

Beck's book *The Beck Diet Solution* about stopping and thinking of the aftermath, and how you'll feel about yourself if you eat something unnecessary. Marion felt it could be developed further, encouraging clients to weigh up the two scenarios – the feelings and consequences of eating, and also of not eating, and comparing how you'd feel in both cases.

It became clear during this development phase of treatment that our clients would benefit from a method of literally freezing time, allowing them to slow down events and really consider the outcomes and consequences of their actions. At the time, this of course related almost exclusively to food and eating. And PBT proved to be a near-perfect 'tool', enabling clients to avoid sabotaging their efforts to shift excess weight by providing a 'safe zone' for considering the consequences. The introduction of a visual aid – a tangible 'remote control' device along the lines of a credit card – enabled clients to continue to build on what they had learned in the G*m*B sessions.

Marion says she can't honestly remember *how* she came up with the progression to a mental remote control device, but that's exactly what she did:

> *'I wanted people not just to stop themselves "in the act", but to pursue the idea so they would be able to visualize themselves in five minutes' time. First of all, if they had gone ahead and eaten a bar of chocolate, and then if they hadn't. In that way they could compare the consequences of their actions. Because I thought it was important to strengthen clients' experience of the two options they were weighing up, I was imagining them visually – and the concept seemed so like using a TV remote that I kept thinking about the possibilities. Martin*

and I brainstormed and tweaked, and figured ways to incorporate all the main remote buttons, and that's how PBT was born!'

We suggest to clients that they visualize themselves at a fork in the road. Having pressed Pause, they give themselves thinking time to consider what's along the 'good road' and what's down the 'bad road', depending on what they choose to do about that bar of chocolate (plate of chips, whatever…) sitting in front of them. This means they then have the time to understand the consequences of their actions and which choice they're actually going to make.

When you're in that situation you can feel helpless, but if you know you have the ability in other areas of your life to be controlled and think logically, you should be able to use it right *now*, in this moment. What you need is the ability to see beyond the moment; to look past the 'right here, right now' way of thinking. You've got to see everything that will result – the aftermath. PBT is a way of actually stopping for a second – or as long as you need – and thinking through the consequences of how you're going to react.

You can't change what's happened in the past, but you can learn from past mistakes, then draw a line under the past, focus on the present and change how you're about to react right now. As a result, you will see different, more positive consequences in the future.

Our clinic has never focused exclusively on weight issues – we have always seen clients with other problems, addictions and panic attacks being just two examples. The seed of the thought that PBT could have *much* wider uses came – as do so many good ideas – more by accident than design.

A client having sessions to deal with anger management was with Martin for his weekly visit and idly picked up a Pause Button card left on the coffee table by a previous client. He asked what it was, and so Martin explained its use in weight loss, and how it could possibly be used in other areas of treatment. With that in mind, the client asked to take it home. He returned the following week saying how useful it had been in helping him 'Pause' himself before choosing inappropriately angry reactions or responses.

And that, simple though it may be, was the start of a brand new, stand-alone therapy, incorporated into the treatment plans for clients with a range of problems and conditions. It has been used successfully with cocaine addiction and panic attacks, and in relationship counselling.

As time went on, and not without considerable fine-tuning, we incorporated it into our stop smoking, bulimia, depression, road rage and OCD therapy. We soon realized that, in fact, the possibilities seemed endless: any situation that could benefit from a moment or two's extra thought can have just that if you press 'Pause' and follow through the 'Pause-Fast Forward-Rewind-Fast Forward-Play' sequence.

We find that the PBT technique has filled a real gap in situations where clients seem clueless as to how to 'stop' and really consider the implications of the action they are about to take.

Informal discussions with other therapists highlighted a real interest in PBT, and there was general agreement that there was a need for a new, modern, easily understandable approach to so many disorders and emotional problems.

In therapy, possibly even more so than in other walks of life, it is arguably true to say that the more techniques, systems, 'tools', therapies and approaches available, the greater the chance of finding a method to suit every client. After all, everyone's different and everyone's problems, and their effects on their lives, will be different.

From assisting with deep-seated psychological problems to providing simple tools for people with behaviours and habits they wanted to change, the benefits could spread significantly. As we'll explain, there's a case to be made for introducing PBT within public health. Could GPs save time and avoid prescribing certain drugs if people just learned to press Pause?

Schools, too – where we increasingly hear of ill-discipline, bullying, truancy and a general lack of motivation affecting the education of our children – could benefit from even brief training in PBT.

If counsellors trained to deal with unruly youngsters had a technique that all school kids already understood – arguably better than most adults – how much better might classroom behaviour become? If bullies were taught to press Pause and think about the consequences of their actions, wouldn't that have a positive knock-on effect for more than one family?

We know from initial studies how effective the method is. Educationalist Gay Jones deals with this in a later chapter, explaining how the techniques have been used in trials in a number of UK primary schools. Gay, who has taken up a role in this aspect of PBT International, has fine-tuned and headed up the development of training modules for teachers and others involved in schools, who will then be able to introduce PBT straight into the classroom.

Of course it needn't just be schools, or young people's behaviour in question. How about prisons? What if persistent offenders were required to agree to be trained in PBT before being allowed out on probation? How much re-offending might that reduce? How much prison space might it free up? How many would-be victims might it remove from statistics?

In fact, how many problems, issues and illnesses *wouldn't* be helped by the input of a touch of PBT at the appropriate moment?

Anyone can grasp the idea of a remote control, or visualization, in minutes. The same can't be said of CBT, which takes quite a bit longer to explain to clients.

We recommend that people using the PBT technique either obtain a PBT card and/or one of our wristbands (available at www.pausebuttontherapy.com), visualize one of the devices or use the 'crooked finger' technique. These are described in the following pages.

The PBT card and wristband

The PBT Sequence

Throughout the book we describe the sequence in which you begin by pausing the moment, then visualizing the potential results of what you are about to do; thinking through your options and finally making a decision before taking action. The way you do this is up to you, and will vary according to your specific problem and the context in which you usually experience it.

It will help you, though, to have a template, a basic format to follow. It may be easier if, to begin with, we present this as a fictitious but plausible situation.

Graham knows the theory of PBT and has taught himself how to identify his own trigger moments – the ones that have got him into trouble in the past. After work, he calls into a bar with some work colleagues to discuss a problem that arose that day. He orders a small beer, conscious that he's got to drive home.

After 20 minutes one of his colleagues gets up to buy a round of drinks for everybody and, without asking, comes back with another beer for Graham. He's enjoying the conversation and companionship, and the first cold beer had just seemed to glide down his throat. When the second beer unexpectedly appears in front of him, he knows the trigger of old, so, as he's become accustomed to, he just presses Pause in his mind for a few seconds and quickly Fast Forwards to see the first of the two options ahead of him. It's a bit like a 'fork in the road' situation. He can enjoy spending a bit longer with his friends, and the second beer, but when he gets home his wife and children won't be happy because he'd promised he wouldn't be late home from work. Plus, of course, if he got pulled up by the police on his way home and breathalysed, the effect on him and his family could be catastrophic.

To see the other route, he Rewinds and quickly Fast Forwards again, looks at the beer in front of him and visualizes a different option – to pass the beer to his friend beside him, refusing it for himself. He can see himself driving home quite relaxed after the chat with his friends, knowing that he's not at risk of losing his licence. Because he's home early, he also has that precious time to spend with his children before they go to bed.

Now comes the time to Rewind back to the present, make whatever decision is right for him at that particular time, press Play and get on with his evening.

Putting PBT into Your Own Life

So, your template should follow this sequence:

1. Identify the moment; that nano-second when you need to press the Pause button and think, 'Stop.' This is the hardest part. It's learning which situations you need to stop and think about, and which you don't. (We'll go into this in much, much more detail, don't worry!)

2. Press Pause. Now you're safe; nothing can 'get at you', no one can influence you – life has just frozen for as long as you need it to. This may just be a few seconds, or it may be longer.

3. Now use the Fast Forward button to go forward to the future, whether it's an hour or a day. See, smell, and feel the results of what you're about to do to get a clear, full-colour picture of the scene at the time. This allows you to experience in detail the ramifications of what you did or said, whatever it happens to be.

4. Now Rewind back to the present, and then Fast Forward to the second option. Repeat the visualization process and see how much better you feel, how empowered, the positive feelings, the feelings of control.

5. Once again, Rewind to the present, and decide which of the actions you are going to take.

6. Press Play and get on with your life.

Whilst Graham's may be a very simple example, it's what we could all do every day with decisions. It doesn't really matter whether it's about having a second drink, replying to the text that you've just received or reacting to an inappropriate comment by your partner. PBT is all about stopping and thinking about the consequences of your actions or thoughts, with ramifications that could go on for months into the future.

Simply having the sequence written out, the template as explained above, is not enough. Don't allow yourself to believe you can stop reading here. Changing behaviour takes time, and recognizing the full significance of the Pause, understanding why you need to visualize consequences and seeing how your thought processes are important are all key and need to be thoroughly addressed. We will expand on all these, and more, in the following chapters. You could sum PBT up in four words:

Pause... Think... Decide... Act

'The card empowers the user to make more informed choices about their own actions and lives.'
MARTIN SHIRRAN

A PAUSE BUTTON MOMENT

Tanya was at work when she received a sharply worded email from her ex-husband saying he was too busy to have the children as planned. He knew she wasn't supposed to get private emails at work. He knew it was his weekend with the children. She felt her temper rising and picked up her mobile, ready to text him back. Words were flowing round her head; what to call him, how cross and exasperated she was at his attitude to child access. Maybe it would be better to email, even if she shouldn't? More space to really tell him what she thought.

Thankfully, though, her PBT training kicked in as she'd practised… rather than sending a hasty, provocative message, she was able to press Pause and go into her safe zone. From there she could take her own time to press Fast Forward and see the possible consequences of her actions. If she sent an angry email, her boss might well get to know she'd been using the system without permission. That wouldn't be great for her job prospects. Her ex-husband would become even angrier, and when he did eventually agree to see the children (which wasn't going to be this weekend, from the sound of it), he'd probably be grumpy with them as well as with her.

Having pressed Rewind, she then went on Fast Forward again to see the alternative course of action. She'd calmed down and sent him a reasonable message, explaining how disappointed the children would be, which he'd read and realize maybe he'd been a bit hasty and that he could tweak other arrangements to fit in with his children. The weekend went ahead as originally planned… and Tanya's job was under no threat at all.

No contest, really. Having taken the time to see both sets of consequences, she made her decision and pressed Play.

IN THIS CHAPTER YOU'VE LEARNED:

- Such a simple concept.
- You've got a remote control at home, haven't you? You know how to use it.
- Yes, this book could change your life… with your help!

*Pause * Think * Decide * Act*

2

A CLOSER LOOK
AT PBT IN USE

*'If we are to learn to improve the quality of the
decisions we make, we need to accept the
mysterious nature of our snap judgements.'*
**MALCOLM GLADWELL, *BLINK: THE POWER OF
THINKING WITHOUT THINKING*, 2005**

In so many – probably all – of the situations we'll be dealing
with in this book, the action/reaction time is minimal. In the
case of alcohol, or food, or drugs, the period you'd be 'enjoying'
them in afterwards would be very short, too. Think about it: if all
you're looking at is short-lived, instant gratification, what better
than a 'virtual' remote control for your life so you can physically
freeze-frame and give yourself time for a mental (and probably
literal) deep breath?

By physically pausing, weight-loss clients achieve two
things that will be equally applicable to anyone reading this
book in addressing different problems. On the one hand, they
give themselves the opportunity to look at the consequences
of their actions – the result of eating their 'trigger' food, or the
better result of not eating it. But they also give themselves the

time and space to realize that *not* eating that trigger food won't kill them. (Of course, although they can't see it at the time, in the longer term, that food is just as likely to kill them as depriving themselves of it feels like it will kill them at the time!) What they most need to see, though, is that they *can* get through the next five minutes without collapsing in a heap. They just need to hit Pause, stop and think of the consequences!

Instant Gratification

Why do so many of us have the 'gut' requirement for instant gratification? Might it be because, historically, our lives needed a far greater reliance on speedy responses – whether to attack, to obtain food that others might take if we didn't, to save our children and protect our heritage…? Essentially, for thousands of years mankind needed to react instantaneously for survival.

We can hardly say that of the 21st century (nor the 20th, for that matter, nor a fair while back from then!). And by retaining our inbuilt preference for instant gratification, we're doing ourselves no good whatsoever. We really ought to take a look at the bigger picture at every available opportunity, to see if we actually need to react/respond in the way we're inclined to. The way we're suggesting, of course, is by pressing Pause and freezing your life and illogical thoughts for just a moment or two.

Let's translate this to a different behaviour, a different problem: unwanted pregnancy.

By pressing Pause when about to have spur-of-the-moment sex, you give yourself a chance to think through the consequences. In the case of pregnancy, those truly would be far-reaching. Take a breath and really consider it. Zoom in and peer closely at what will happen. Try to see the whole thing played out in slow motion. Your studies or your career would be severely disrupted. Your income stream possibly cut to nothing. Your family embroiled in possible child-care and financial assistance. The other person's family, ditto. And children remain dependent on their parents for a good many years, so the knock-on effect of that one sexual encounter could last a lifetime. Rewind, Fast Forward to having delayed the deed long enough to consider your motivation, behave mindfully, buy a condom, or even think better of the whole episode, and your life needn't have changed one iota. Rewind, make a decision and Play. So what have you decided to do?

Staying with 21st-century lifestyle choices, do you have a tattoo? Does anyone you know have one? Do they now regret it? For sure, there are plenty of people who have given long and careful consideration to putting needle-applied artwork on their skin and, for them, there are probably few regrets apart from their choice of font, or which tattooist they used.

How many others, though, made a snap decision on a night out, waltzed into a tattoo parlour and came out marked for life?

Do people – the average Joe on the street – think hard enough about how the naked woman on their forearm will look later in life, when their skin's older, wrinkled, maybe fat and stretched?

Martin sees this as just another example of prime Pause Button territory. He speaks of wealthy 50-something females who had tattoos done when they were younger – you see them on the beach, their tattoos in very prominent positions. They just couldn't have thought that through. They needed to take a deep breath, press Pause and consider all the consequences.

Did those people really think about how they'd look when they were 10, 20, 30 or 40 years older? They've got other body issues to fret about when they're in their fifties, but Martin is sure they think to themselves, 'This tattoo was a mistake.'

It's not only 'ordinary' people who sometimes have to admit that the decision to have a tattoo might not have been wise. Bob Geldof's daughter Peaches had her first tattoo at 14 and is quoted as saying she regrets every single one she's had. She is understood to have said that if she could graft a new skin for herself, she would.[1]

Film star Angelina Jolie had the name of ex-husband Billy Bob Thornton tattooed on her left arm. When the relationship failed she needed painful laser surgery to rid her of the now less-than-happy memory.[2]

Martin knows one young woman who has been determined since she was a teenager to have a tattoo. Her parents acted as her Pause Button 'monitors' and she actually listened! She did eventually get a tattoo, but far smaller than she had originally planned, and not in plain view. Her mum says their thoughts were of consequences: future jobs, employers, attitudes, the whole thing. They pressed Pause on her behalf and this triggered her change!

The final word goes to someone with a tattoo. Would most people think through all the possible consequences of having one? 'I'd have to say, most of the time, no,' she says.

Moving seamlessly from ink-stained skin to piercings, have you ever wondered if everyone with anything more extreme than pierced ears actually thought before going ahead?

It would be easy to come across as negative or judgemental... that's not our intention at all. The intention, as with the whole of the rest of this book, is to alert you, dear reader, to the consequences that result from your every decision.

So, in the case of piercings, if your decision is to have one, you should press Pause and imagine all the possible outcomes, which may in turn depend on the location of your chosen piercing. On just one of many websites on the subject is a list of 52 possible 'locations' on the body, 35 of which are visible (i.e., not concealed by clothing).[3] Until recently, companies often had 'dress codes' for employees and were able to specify permitted levels of makeup and jewellery. Although the litigation culture has played a part in changing this, you may like to consider if the existence of visible piercings could affect your chances in the jobs market…

Returning to the critically important visual imagery provided by PBT, the mental image of a remote control, reinforced by using your thumb and your crooked forefinger, or Pause Button device/wristband if you have one to hand, means you can easily perform any of the functions of a remote control device. You can go on Fast Forward and then Pause to see yourself (in the case of a hastily sent text, for example) having had that instant adrenaline rush of metaphorically beating the person up for whatever it was that riled you. Great feeling, eh? Then go on to five minutes *after* you've finished and press Play again – what's going to be going through your head then? Will you be feeling guilty, beating yourself up and thinking 'Why on Earth did I do that? What will they think of me? I'll never be able to look them in the eye again. I'm just not in control.'

Then Rewind back to the present and run the film through in your head again, but this time add in the nice 'happy ever after' ending and see yourself making the right choice. How much better do you feel about yourself in that scenario?

Motivation can be very easily defined as the 'Why' of life. *Why* eat so much you can barely stand up then make yourself sick? *Why* decide to buy that handbag when you know perfectly well you've eight others at the bottom of the wardrobe? *Why* have that drink when you know it will put you over the limit?

That's one for you to ponder, really... the 'Why' of what it is you do. More relevant to change, though, is *Why* should you alter your behaviour?

Establish what your motivation is and you're halfway there. Probably more than halfway. If you want to achieve something, fair enough. That's one thing. If you want to achieve it for X, Y or Z reason, and that's sufficient to get you really moving along the road, then it counts as true motivation.

What will make you do things differently? Instead of just *thinking* about doing things differently... would it be having enough motivation to persuade you to take action?

Some of these might be sufficient:

- I don't want to end up in trouble with the police.
- It's about time I stopped kidding myself that I only gamble occasionally.
- I'm fed up with being the only parent at school who smells like an ashtray.
- I don't want to develop Type 2 diabetes.
- I can't afford to keep spending on stupid impulse buys.
- I want to keep my job because my family depend on me. My addiction might get me fired.

- I don't want alcohol to control the rest of my life.
- I hate myself when I scream at the kids; they're young and need me to be a loving mum.
- I don't want to lose my licence on a drink-drive charge.
- I want my family to stop worrying about me.
- I'm fed up of being out of control.
- I want to look and feel sexy in nice clothes again.
- I want my children to be proud of me.
- I want to get to 40 (or 30, or 50) without this cloud of fat or haze of booze hanging over me.
- I don't want to damage my skin/liver/kidneys/heart through my over-consumption.
- I know I want to be a different me.

Pausing will be the tool to provide the safe zone, the thinking time, the opportunity to Fast Forward and reflect on what you'd really like to be feeling and thinking, in 10 minutes, 10 weeks or whatever. Motivation is maybe what will help you make those hopes and desires achievable. Why not spend a moment or two deciding what your motivations are?

If you reverse Milton H. Erickson's quote, 'A goal without a date is just a dream', you could regard a goal as a dream with a 'do by' date.

Everyone knows of situations in which numbers of people want to achieve something, while only a few actually do. Sportspeople are classic examples of this. So what's different about those who make it? What's different about the people who succeed?

It's their commitment, their motivation, seeing the end picture, and their sheer belief that it's possible. You see, that *belief* is a big thing, isn't it? If you allow yourself to think you're not likely to succeed, you're setting yourself up for failure. People have really got to visualize that success. Use all their senses. Believe and there's a much greater chance you'll achieve.

It's no coincidence that the words 'see' and 'visualize' keep cropping up. The remote control device is mainly associated with DVDs, TVs and video players. What you might not know is just how visual a species the human race is. Much of the way we learn about our world – judge, adjust, even simply enjoy – is done using visual means.

As humans, we see things in pictures. We are predisposed to think things through, or imagine them, visually; it comes naturally. That's why film is such a powerful medium. It keys in straight away to the way our brains think.

The fact that we think in metaphor is the most powerful aspect of this visual sense. Metaphor is a visual language that's very powerful. Consider advertising: you only have to see a colour to start thinking of brands associated with that colour...

We are deeply affected by images. Film is an evocative medium; TV has established itself slap bang in the heart of global culture. What better way to bring home to yourself the folly of your intended action than by literally 'seeing' it through to its conclusion, good or bad, when you put yourself on Pause?

The really quite short timescale required to go through the Pause-Fast Forward-Rewind-Pause-Fast Forward-Rewind-Play sequence fits in fairly accurately with most impulse scenarios.

Take the case of food – some people are already beating themselves up within moments of putting food in their mouths.

When Martin first started looking at the scope for broadening the use of PBT into other disorders and behaviours, he'd had limited 'hands-on' experience of the therapy because Marion is the one who runs those specific sessions within their GmB work. He soon saw, though, how easy it would be to adapt the theory to deal with virtually any scenario.

Stopping before a thought is translated into an action is critical with addictions, which Martin feels pretty much always involve an element of planning. Cigarettes... The smoker has to plan to have enough to 'get through' a drive, or a party, or whatever. Drugs... The person has to find a dealer, meet up with him or her, buy the drugs, etc. If you can stop them at the beginning of the first thought, you stand a chance of stopping the thought before it's carried through to an action.

You want someone who suffers with road rage to use the Pause Button in the morning, when he realizes he's already agitated about the drive. Then he'll know the implications of his anger, and know to calm himself down.

The university student going out drinking – they'll maybe be thinking, 'Am I going to meet a girl tonight, is there a chance I'm going to have sex, am I prepared?' Then, having pressed Pause, they can take themselves through the possible implications of unprotected sex – STDs, unwanted pregnancy and more – and start thinking about these in advance!

> *'Good decisions come from experience,*
> *and experience comes from bad decisions.'*
> **Anonymous**

It might seem unrealistic to expect everyone who's ever made a hasty decision to see the need for such an 'early warning' Pause, but there's a point to be learned every time you try it. If you Pause and think before making a judgement call, even if you don't choose the 'best' option, the next time you are faced with a choice it's more likely you'll use the Pause idea again. And every time you try it, it becomes more implanted as a technique to use. So someday you'll be able to Pause far earlier, and predict your own triggers far more accurately.

You'll also learn that, just because something has always happened a particular way in the past, it doesn't mean history will repeat itself. You do have the ability to take control now, in the present. You *can* do something different, and get a different outcome. This is a very empowering lesson. You are the one in control.

Of course, many, possibly all, of the behaviours we'll be looking at in this book can be described in totally different terms through the CBT 'lens'. This suggests there are ways our mind convinces us to believe things that aren't true. These are known as negative automatic thoughts, which are flawed, illogical, sabotaging thoughts that can have a monumentally negative effect on people if they're allowed to.

Dealing with Sabotaging Thoughts

Sabotaging thoughts fall into the following self-explanatory sub-groups:

- All or nothing thinking (perfectionism)
- Discounting the positive
- Jumping to conclusions

- Emotional reasoning
- Self-deluding thinking
- Confusing wants with needs
- Over-generalization (sweeping statements)

Recognizing these patterns of illogical thinking, and combining that understanding with the use of your Pause Button technique, means you will have the tools to deal with almost any negative feelings that come up.

Anxiety

Can you deal with the change you're facing? Are you going to permit anxious behaviour to take over? Well, Pause yourself, Fast Forward down one route of uncertainty and spiralling negativity – the consequences of which could be anything from depression and anger to poor performance at work – then Rewind and Fast Forward to the other choice of behaviour, to see and feel how much happier, more positive, your present day could be if you just 'talk' your way mentally out of these illogical thoughts.

Fear

Follow the same pattern through: fear is often unfounded, constructed from any blend of sabotaging thoughts, exaggerated thinking and so on.

Threat

This could be rooted in concern about potential reactions from other people to the 'new' you. Will they be disillusioned? Just follow the PBT routes as described.

Guilt

Has your previous behaviour left you with shame or guilt about the consequences of your actions? Work your way through the technique again. Not allowing guilt to take over is positive. Better still, you know you're not likely to feel guilty again because you're dealing with your flawed behaviours. Positivity again!

And never forget, avoiding 'fortune telling' is all about living in the present!

Personal change can be really hard, and things don't change overnight. We often don't realize the importance of this, but being able to live in the present is an essential skill. Sometimes, people need to understand themselves more to be able to do this – to understand why they feel the way they do, why they act the way they do and how they cope. Knowing how the past has influenced today can comfort some and help them to work through it. Understanding themselves as a whole – their fears, failures, hopes and dreams – can only assist them in the moment. Knowing yourself helps you in the present – don't you think? Pause Button Therapy could be a key factor in helping you live in the present appreciating what is happening today, and realizing which of your thoughts may be influenced by past events. As we also highlight elsewhere, simply thinking and acting mindfully is another method of achieving this.

Most people go into therapy because they are either living in/with their past or catastrophically thinking about their future, maybe both. PBT allows you to live in the present and consider your options and the consequences of your actions. If we can find a way to stay in the present moment, massive changes often happen in our lives.

In the end, though, a thought can only take up as much space in your head as you allow it to. If you recognize a sabotaging thought for what it is, you have the power and control to stop it in its tracks right there and then if you want to, or you can choose to allow it to build up out of all proportion. So, whatever the outcome, it really is your own choice. You will begin to recognize that you are the one who is in control, and you can decide what the outcome is going to be, depending on how you react to any given situation or stimulus.

Never forget, either, just how empowering that belief in your own self-control can be. We see it as a kind of perpetual motion, an upward spiral of confidence. All this comes from knowing that you, yes *you*, can, if you choose, achieve something you set your mind to.

Ultimately, we do believe there comes a time (chosen by the individual – who are we to say when someone is ready?!) when a person feels ready to take responsibility for themselves, for today. They need to choose to learn to live for today, in the present.

> *'As a rule, men worry more about what they can't see than about what they can.'*
> JULIUS CAESAR

Maybe, before going a single page further in a book about Pausing, we should do exactly that – Pause – and have a look at the word!

Merely looking at the word 'Pause' can take you on quite a path of discovery – of the English language, of course, but also to realizing the different connotations, implications and inferences that the many and various alternatives provide. Yet all of these contain that one essential, core value: a cessation of action. These are just some of the definitions of the word Pause in various dictionaries. Not all of them, by a long chalk![4]

- Break
- Breathe
- Breather
- Breathing space
- Catch one's breath
- Cease
- Delay
- Deliberate
- Half-time
- Halt
- Freeze
- Gap
- Halt
- Have a breather
- Hold
- Interrupt
- Interval
- Rest
- Take a break
- Take five
- Time lag

- Time-out
- Wait

Quite a list to ponder!

If you consider other applications of the word Pause, though, you'll see just how helpful, possibly vital, the notion of taking 'Time Out' is if you're to live a mindful life rather than one peppered with hit-and-miss judgements, questionable comments and distinctly dodgy decisions.

If you're a public speaker, a pause in the right spot can mean the difference between a forgotten speech and a world-famous quote. A classic of its type is John F. Kennedy's now unforgettable sound bite, 'And so, my fellow Americans, ask not what your country can do for you; ask what you can do for your country.' Not really unforgettable written like that, is it?! However, read it again with the pause he actually inserted: 'And so, my fellow Americans, ask not what your country can do for you;'... *Pause...* 'ask what you can do for your country.'

It gives emphasis, of course, but more than that, it gives the listener 'thinking time' to consider what was said first and what was the follow-up. So similar to using the Pause Button!

A PAUSE BUTTON MOMENT

Maggie would visit the supermarket weekly to buy a scratchcard; she found that she was quite lucky. Somewhere along the line, though, the one a week started to become one every day. When she saw the effect on her bank balance, she started buying even more in the hope of finding that elusive winning ticket. Within six months her gambling habit was completely out of control; it was having a real effect on the housekeeping budget and she was constantly afraid her husband would find out. One day, in desperation, she started surfing the internet looking for help with her gambling, and came across a forum that talked about PBT.

In the supermarket the very next day, she pressed the Pause Button and visualized the consequences of spending yet another £20 on scratchcards. The effects of the deceit on her marriage. Then she somehow managed to press Fast Forward and realized straight away that if she walked away from the cashier she would feel empowered, as though she had taken back control. Within just a few weeks she had got back to the situation where she was treating herself to just one scratchcard, bought on a Friday on the way home from work.

IN THIS CHAPTER YOU'VE LEARNED:

- Developing the PBT technique.
- Mind-reading, fortune telling and other automatic thoughts.
- Visualizing consequences.

*Pause * Think * Decide * Act*

PART 2

CONSIDERING CONSEQUENCES

3

PBT IN YOUR HANDS

'When anger rises, think of the consequences.'
CONFUCIUS

OK, so how is this any more than just a gimmick? Because we wouldn't blame you for saying that's all it is: a few clever phrases and some words incredibly familiar to most people under 35, and that's it...

But actually, no, that's not it by a long way. Sure, you could just say to yourself, 'Stop. Think.' That might help you live a happier, less stressful life. But if you're always getting yourself in trouble, or you've made many poor choices, over-thought yourself into so many depressed times in your life, drunk so many bottles of wine you knew you shouldn't have, shouted at the kids on way too many occasions, allowed yourself to get in the grip of one or other addiction; even had a 'near miss' unwanted pregnancy scare (or known someone who has), you're probably in need of a bit more than that.

PBT *is* about stopping and thinking, but more than that, it's about stopping, taking yourself into the future so you fully see, feel and understand the consequences of your actions, and realizing that (only) *you* hold the key to choosing the right path.

And although that takes much longer to explain than do, it's important to understand the need to follow the process through thoroughly. See the possible outcomes in full Technicolor in your head, and then (and maybe *only* then) you will stand a far better chance of making better choices.

This depth of recognition of the consequences, something we will be emphasizing over and over, is critical to the process of PBT. It's why we incorporate Guided Imagery into our system. Although the use of visual images is important, it's only one of the various elements that combine to have a powerful effect, focusing your imagination and mobilizing your unconscious; strengthening your motivation to achieve whatever outcome you hope for.

Our minds don't really understand the difference between images and real events. We read a recipe book and our mouths water. We've 'seen' our own pictures of the food, 'smelled' its aromas, 'felt' its textures. None of this is real, of course, but the ability the mind has to trigger the body is a bit like a chain reaction: imagination − focused energy/motivation − inspiring more images − greater focus − and so on. We recall our pride, our sense of self-worth, when we remember a particular teacher who oversaw our greatest successes. When revisiting that memory, it's as if we were just bound to do well![1]

In the same way as when we meditate, or are in deep relaxation under hypnosis, Guided Imagery can bring about a sense of altered consciousness. In other words, when you've Fast Forwarded to 'see' how you feel, experiencing the results of poor choices or better ones, the very nature of that visual and other sensory imagery almost wipes out the present moment, and concentrates your mind on identifying what is most important to you.

What's Your Goal?

Maybe most important of all is the realization that using Guided Imagery is our choice. Making a choice, a choice to choose, in itself empowers you because no one else told you to do it. You are in control. And that knowledge that you've taken control is a self-fulfilling prophecy. Control breeds confidence, which breeds optimism and self-esteem. These further empower us to achieve where, previously, with diminished confidence resulting from a lack of control and pessimism (resulting in a lower sense of self-esteem), we would not cope anywhere near as well.

What you might accurately call a virtuous circle!

All actions start with a thought. It might be, 'Hey, snooker's on TV this afternoon; I'm going to miss it *again*.' (Why don't I just phone in sick? I'm not going to worry what my boss will think of me, and he won't remember this when it comes to considering my promotion.)

Or, 'That *#*!#* driver just cut in front of me!' (I will tailgate him, endangering my life and his, running the risk of a ticket, raising my blood pressure, using excess fuel and not getting home any faster as a result – and of course taking my stress out on my nearest and dearest into the bargain.)

Or, 'Why did my husband blank that loving text I sent an hour ago?' (I figure it's because he's being deliberately awkward and rejecting my affections, and when I next need to text him I'll make an issue of it, escalating things despite only *assuming* I know his reasons for not responding.)

Do any of those sound familiar? For all three there are countless variations: different scenarios, different details for each person experiencing that rush of illogical thoughts which leads them by the nose to make bad choices. Behind it? Everything begins with a thought. Every time you behave in a certain way, you're reacting to a trigger. This trigger could be something going on around you, or it could be an internal trigger – a thought. Even if it is an external trigger, behind it there'll still be a thought and, following that, the almost inevitable chain reaction.

Think Before You Act

*'People make mistakes. We are allowed to make mistakes.
But the actions we take while in a rage will haunt us forever.
Pause and ponder. Think before you act. Be patient.'*[2]
MOTHER TERESA

You might not always be conscious of having that thought, or it could be so fleeting as to be imperceptible. Over in an instant. You've had the reaction and you think, 'Goodness, where did that come from?' But if you trace it back, given the time within PBT, you'll realize a thought is always there in the background.

As we've said, for every one of these illogical, knee-jerk thoughts, there will be countless others. But for each and every one, the essential PBT process is the same: The moment you get the rush of anger, adrenaline, fear, craving, you need to put your life on hold by pressing Pause.

As an aside (another aside…), did you ever sit down and figure out that anger can result from frustration? Aggravation? Annoyance? Animosity? Do you really consider that any of these is worth the hassle that uncontrolled anger brings?[3]

For some of you, there's a good chance that simply putting yourself on Pause will be sufficient on its own, with no need to do anything more than simply stop your knee-jerk reaction getting the better of you. If that's the case, a deep breath – really slow, really calming, and as meditative as you can muster – will be what you should strive for. Press Pause, and inhale *slowly* through your nose. If you can, perhaps shut your eyes and visualize your favourite place, where you feel totally at peace. Staying there in that happy, safe place in your mind for a few moments might give you enough time to just re-consider your 'nearly' over-reaction, without the need to look at what would happen if you *did* lose your cool, or your battle with the craving for a cigarette, or your fight to avoid sending that crabby text message.

You might just have needed to Pause and breathe, without doing any more thinking about the knock-on consequences of your actions. But we feel that, to get the best from the Pause Button technique, you should do just that. Pause and think through what would happen. Feel how you would feel. Imagine how your family and friends would feel. See what their faces would look like, hear their voices. Imagine how people might react. Not only will you begin to recognize that the knock-on effect of each of those consequences is cumulative, you will very probably start the process of living a more considerate, mindful, thoughtful life for the benefit of you and all who know you!

Back to the sequence, though. All these side effects and consequences have a bearing on the picture in your mind when you run through your PBT sequence.

You need to look at what will happen (the consequences) if you act in different ways, by pressing Pause-Fast Forward-Rewind-Pause-Fast Forward-Rewind. Then you need to decide which consequence you'd prefer in your life *now*, and press Play.

This will be the start of your journey into allowing your present moment to be lived differently, and better!

The first hurdle to overcome, though, is perhaps an unexpected one: you need to start to understand your own thought processes. By doing that you increase your chances of 'intercepting' your own bad choices – leaping between the thought and the action, or cutting yourself off at the pass, if you like! On top of that, you will be in a better position to understand the nature of the thought processes that blight the lives of so many people with behavioural and addictive disorders that are not so very different from your own problems and issues.

> *'It's not the situation… it's your reaction to the situation.'*
> **BOB CONKLIN**

We said earlier, and will definitely say again – everything *begins* with a thought. Author Richard Carlson helped us to start looking in more depth at that point in his useful book *Stop Thinking, Start Living.*[4] He suggests that a thought is just that: a thought. A transitory nothingness, in all practical senses. Our thoughts are something we can *choose* to act on, re-think, over-think or totally ignore – it's our *choice*.

So those momentary, instantaneous, potentially transient thoughts that we grab on to for dear life and run with – allowing ourselves to get embroiled in all manner of dodgy choices, like playing truant from school, or pressing send on that heated email rather than putting it in drafts – could just be acknowledged as merely a thought and then filed as 'ignore'. Simple as that. You just have to recognize the thought as *only* that. A thought. And thinking – apart from the obviously relevant, necessary stuff – can very easily take you away from living and enjoying the present moment.

Thoughts are just thoughts. They're opinions – no more and no less. We should be very careful not to confuse thoughts with facts, which is often done.

Developing that idea, remember those 'sabotaging' or 'negative automatic thoughts', as defined in CBT, in the last chapter? If you give an illogical thought more headroom than it deserves (and obviously, that's absolutely none!), what is likely to happen is that, with every moment spent thinking about it, the thought itself, which isn't a reality or a fact, remember – it's just a thought – takes on greater significance. It's a vicious circle. You think it, and in thinking it you assume it's worth thinking about; you figure it needs more thought and it becomes more 'important', so you think about it some more… and so on.

It's important to see this in context. Let's start with the example of the bullied child.

My son was bullied at school last week. All children in that school must be cruel; he will never make friends and settle in.

Can't you just imagine it? Within moments (and never forget, these moments only really need be milliseconds), what should have remained a passing notion, very speedily dismissed as no more than a sweeping statement you dreamed up based on a small amount of information – if allowed to be thought, and re-thought, and re-thought – will take on a life of its own. You'll be thinking that every day must be terrible for him. You'll be imagining him on his own, or being tormented in the playground. You'll believe he's tearful right now. You'll be thinking how friendless he must be; how he'll never settle at the school. What a waste of space parent you are for putting him in that situation.

What a hopeless head teacher there must be. Wondering where you'll have to move him to…

> 'When people start to think about the consequences of their actions, everything changes. From how we deal with our overdraft and how we speak to our children, to our fear of the dentist, every time we think of the consequences of our actions everything in our life changes in a heartbeat. We can take control – if we choose to.'
> **MARTIN SHIRRAN**

If you go down that road – and if you're reading this book you probably have done in some scenario or other, not only thinking too little, but at times using valuable minutes and hours of your life over-thinking your way to disaster – what are the chances you'll be thinking of hotfooting it to school to have a run-in with some unsuspecting parent or teacher? And all based on that passing thought which should have been binned several minutes ago.

Now let's put PBT into the mix!

If you have a tendency to overthink things, and then overreact, the moment your child tells you he's been bullied you should press Pause. Use the next few moments to take yourself Fast Forward to consider what knock-on effects *you* and *your* actions would have on him if you went down to give the parents/school a piece of your mind. You would very probably get yourself told off by the staff, or become embroiled in a fairly heated argument with one or more sets of parents. This would not ease your son's school life, and would potentially add in quite a major way to his embarrassment and discomfort levels. Realize how unnecessary – and unnecessarily painful – that would be. Then press Rewind and Fast Forward again to see what would happen if you just took a different approach.

*'The world we have created is a product of
our thinking; it cannot be changed without
changing our thinking.'*
ALBERT EINSTEIN

What if you were simply to stop for a minute and avoid this 'over-generalization' thinking? Say you decided to just have a quiet chat with the teacher next time you were at the school. This route would find you thinking nothing worse, nothing more painful than, 'It's sad he was bullied, but I'm certain not all children at his school are like that.' You may very well have a chat with him about it, with no pressure on him from your almost-aggressive visit to his school. You would be calm enough to help him feel better. A much more positive way of thinking. So now you can Rewind, make your choice of which way to go, and press Play. At which point, all the thinking and over-thinking is over, and you – and your son – can get on with life.

It might seem like a major contradiction to be talking about encouraging *more* thoughtful consideration of the consequences of your actions, while at the same time saying you're very likely guilty of contributing to your problems by *over*-thinking things. Never forget the old adage that refers to 'Decision paralysis by over-analysis'! Make no mistake, though, they're both possible: needing to think more and needing to think less. Both are possible at one and the same time. It depends on the priority given to illogical thought as opposed to rational thought. Identifying when you've moved from one process to the other just takes a Pause!

*'Remember, today is the tomorrow
you worried about yesterday.'*
DALE CARNEGIE

Let's think about the person who's been going through a bit of a hard time lately. Depression — that big black cloud circling overhead — colours just about every action, every decision, every day. The slightest setback takes on a life of its own.

A large percentage of the things we worry about never actually happen yet we spend so much time worrying about them. With a depressed person, this is even more powerful. It all takes on a disproportionate significance.

Our man is off to an overseas business meeting — fearful he'll forget his tickets, panicking about the timetables, unsure whether or not there'll be time to plan his presentation before he arrives. In a clearer frame of mind he would know he had actually organized his time relatively efficiently, and had all his key points written down, almost remembered. But the big black cloud alters his view. He feels second-rate. As if some kind of weight is on his shoulders.

If only he'd pressed Pause and stopped and thought, Do I have any power to change anything? If not, there's no point worrying about it. Within the safe zone of Pause Button, he's able to look at the facts. Not only the facts about how things are right now, but how things will go if he continues to be negative about everything. Will he give the right impression to the people he's trying to win over? What will their faces be like if he comes into the meeting with no vigour about him, no sense of excitement, purpose, passion for the project? Will they feel he's someone they want to do business with?

In the alternative scenario, he'll see very clearly indeed how much more enthusiastic they will be about his presentation if he's upped his game, come out from under the black cloud and really put on a positive demonstration of his abilities.

Previously, he'd have been thinking that every little glitch seemed unimaginably bad. Now he can see that idea is based on the square root of zilch.

So, do you have your motivation? Have you identified your 'Why?' to help you decide? Rewind again, make your choice as to which course to take, whatever the scenario, whatever your behavioural problem. Decide. And press Play.

> *'We are what we think.'*
> **BUDDHA**

Success as a Sliding Scale

When it comes to habits, it's worth pointing something out. With drinking and smoking, and in fact quite a lot of behaviours that may or may not have reached the point of addiction, it's often the case that it takes more than one attempt to stop. For example, some people try to give up smoking up to a dozen or so times before finally quitting. If you use Pause Button techniques you may indeed not succeed in making that one beer the last ever, or that cigarette your final one. You may not even want to; you might just want to cut down. Now that would be an achievement! *So*, if you think about the consequences of drinking, or consider what smoking is doing to your health and bank balance as a result of pressing Pause, or frankly give any level of serious thought to the possibility of stopping, that's obviously a good thing.

If somebody smokes 40 cigarettes a day and after three weeks they still haven't managed to stop smoking, but now they're smoking five a day – one in the morning, one after lunch, one with afternoon tea, one after dinner and one before they go to bed – has the therapy been a success or a failure? It's been an amazing success.

They could use it before giving up, to give themselves the chance to stop and think about the benefits of being a non-smoker. How much more energy they'll have, how much more ability to run up and down stairs without getting breathless, reducing their risk of lung cancer, reducing their risk of heart disease – all by using their Pause moment to see the benefits.

Someone having a cigarette is thinking about right now, not about the future consequence of what they're doing. PBT works as a stand-alone tool to help people move straight to where they want to be, but it also works as a tool to help them get one stage closer.

If PBT moves someone from not having tried to stop to cutting down, or at least thinking about it, that's one stage nearer giving up. It may not be what the textbooks want, but this is the real world. The person's finally starting to get a degree of control. Never forget how important regaining control can be – remember the virtuous circle!

In a later chapter we will take a close look at the Model of Change, which describes the processes we go through when attempting any change in life.

'You may have to fight a battle more than once to win it.'
MARGARET THATCHER

A Multi-layered Approach

If you look at most of the stories in your morning paper today, apart from natural disasters there probably aren't many for which PBT couldn't have made – or maybe still could make – a difference. Out of interest, we'll take that look in another chapter to demonstrate exactly what we mean!

The types of events that could have had a totally different outcome vary hugely in intensity or significance. Family stresses and strains may not match up to an unwanted teen pregnancy. Football managers' pitch-side argy-bargy may equate to celebrity meltdowns or inheritance battles… or they may not, depending on whether you're the football manager or the celebrity. It's all down to the individual's perceptions.

Some of these issues can easily be addressed by a person *wanting* to change his behaviour and being *motivated* to work towards change within himself. He may just need a friendly nudge in the right direction. We believe that can be done using the sense of direction, focus and understanding provided by PBT.

Other problems might be sufficiently disabling for the sufferer (or indeed his family) to have sought help from his GP – yet there is still almost limitless scope for PBT to assist. If the person goes to a GP familiar with PBT, it might only need a few weeks to learn and perfect the Pause Button system for him to be able to make a major difference in his life, and even make the next doctor's appointment unnecessary.

There will, of course, be other cases in which PBT serves as a 'holding' technique to help the person cope with their problems more easily while waiting to see the doctor, or being referred on to a counsellor or psychologist.

Which brings us seamlessly to the most complex application – for those with profound behavioural problems. Here, PBT could still be relevant, possibly in the form of self-help, but most likely involving a PBT-trained therapist who can weave 'Press Pause' into deep therapy.

These three 'levels' of using PBT can accurately be described as minor, moderate and severe:

Minor

Sufficient to deal with relatively superficial problems (everyone's problem is important, of course!), such as rethinking hastily-sent texts, not losing your cool with your kids, being more understanding with your other half, kicking the road rage habit, thinking about whether or not to play truant today, not getting into trouble because you can't say no to that one drink too many.

Moderate

The kind of help needed to address a more complex problem, such as giving up smoking, or deep anxiety leading to panic attacks. As with all issues, though, this needs an acceptance that you need to make this change, and/or have chosen to take action in your own interest to make life happier in the present.

Severe

This is more the action of 'last resort', applicable in cases in which an issue is deeply embedded and requires input from health professionals. That doesn't, however, mean the person needing treatment can't have her own constructive input – as we've said before, PBT can be used both by the individual and by a trained therapist or counsellor. In the case of serious behavioural or addictive disorders, such as self-harming, drug abuse, or OCD (Obsessive Compulsive Disorder), PBT is a tool to help those individuals who acknowledge and have a clear understanding of what they're doing to themselves, but haven't quite got to dealing with it. On top of that, though, their counsellor or therapist can use it to help stop their thought processes within and during the therapy process. It can be used to Pause what's happening to them in any given moment within the therapy, and provide the time, maybe the first ever opportunity, to analyze what's going wrong with their thinking.

Between sessions of therapy, PBT is also the perfect 'holding' mechanism to reduce any fear felt by sufferers over periods when they need to cope without the help of their therapist. This in turn is likely to boost their confidence in their ability to control their problem behaviour. As we've said, an example of a truly virtuous PBT circle!

A PAUSE BUTTON MOMENT

A month before he was due to leave prison, Samuel was one of the young repeat offenders chosen to undertake a brief introduction to PBT. The idea of the training was to show these offenders the consequences of their actions once they'd been released, and how just a small deviation from what is deemed right and wrong could have the massive consequence of putting them back behind bars for even longer if there was a 'next time' in court. Samuel believed that, if he'd been introduced to PBT the first time he was sentenced to a term in a Young Offender Institution, he may not have re-offended and ended up in prison again.

IN THIS CHAPTER YOU'VE LEARNED:

- The *virtuous* circle of control.
- Everything starts with a thought.
- Visualizing consequences.

---

*Pause * Think * Decide * Act*

THE INEVITABILITY OF KARMA

*'For every minute you are angry you lose
60 seconds of happiness.'*
RALPH WALDO EMERSON

Arguably more important than understanding where, when and how to use PBT in your own life is the need to understand a fundamental of your, my and everyone else's lives. Though it may seem like a major generalization, we *choose* – every single person chooses – what happens in life by choosing what to say, what to do, how to react, who to spend time with.

We decide who to be nice to, who to lock horns with and, by deciding or opting – ultimately the clearest possible word is *choosing* – how to behave at any given instant in time, we affect what happens as a result. Maybe not from birth, because *choice* of behaviour probably starts somewhere between older childhood and puberty. But let's agree that, between the ages of 8 and 13, people have begun consistently to 'be' a particular way on a moment-by-moment, day-by-day basis. Recognizing that our behaviours, every single one of them, result in consequences, is pretty much the key to shaping our own future.

Say, as an insecure teenager, you chose to spend time with older people who made you feel more mature, more accepted. You began drinking with them after work. You paid little attention to your old school friends. As an adult you started to realize you were, in fact, somewhat lonely, lacking the support network of family, friends and acquaintances that so many other people seem to have.

Way down the line, years into the future, you realize you've few friends left from college – indeed, not too many friends at all; everyone you spend time with is basically just a drinking buddy. You shaped that part of your own future by making those choices, starting as a teenager, didn't you?

Or do you recognize the following? As an 11-year-old you chose to be mean to a classmate – you liked the feeling of being 'important', of being 'big', of being 'hard'; in fact, the feeling of control it gave you. You became something of a bossy boots, graduating to quite a bully, and, as a consequence, once you were identified, you were disliked and marginalized more than you had been attempting to do to your victims.

That feeling of isolation, of not being one of the 'nice' kids with loads of friends, then snowballed into you becoming 'a bit of a loner', someone people didn't automatically gravitate towards. You remained somewhat aggressive, though by now maybe even you could see you had probably created the whole situation by opting for the bullying behaviour in the first place, no?

Or were you the shy, reserved, 'wouldn't say boo to a goose' swot who would rather get on with their homework than be out playing? You opted to do every extra class available. You did everything your parents asked of you. You saw good grades as the Holy Grail and chose to burn the midnight oil to achieve them. When you sat back with your good exam results and nice steady job, did you have a moment wondering what might have become of you if you'd chosen to be a little less studious and a little more gregarious?

Although character traits are undoubtedly part of everyone, there are other elements which are opted for, chosen... and the consequences are there for you to gauge. Don't misinterpret that last example, however. There's nothing wrong with choosing to be a worker rather than a 'loser'. Nothing wrong at all. Unless that choice has led the 'hard worker' to be an unhappy person. Not all are – but those who are, well, it's maybe one of those choice things that would have been better dealt with by using a PBT moment.

As you will read later in Graham's story, consequences can very obviously be cumulative and end up playing a significant part in shaping your life.

PBT may have been developed mainly to help people short-circuit their more instantaneous action/reaction problems, but by seeing the repercussions of a number of those actions, you can judge for yourself all the moments and all the ways in which using PBT could have changed the course of your own past/present, and how it can help you make better choices for yourself in future.

OK, you may struggle to figure out how sending a less-than-polite text to your line manager at work will have an impact on your personal life 10 or 15 years down the line, but think 'butterfly effect.' You send that text. OK, all you actually said was what everyone was thinking: 'Happy Christmas, Matthew, so good to see you enjoying the party SOOOOOO much with Tina from accounts! Jingle B@lls!'

Well – and no surprise here – the line manager takes exception. You've made him feel stupid, out of control. His wife has access to his phone. That's not what he wants her to read.

Make no mistake: you will be paying for this, and soon. You get a dressing-down, and he is now primed to leap on your next transgression with greater force. By now, your family knows you were a bit of a wally doing what you did, so they tease you mercilessly. Any slightly ill-judged decision, any misspelled text or email, gets poked fun at. Your friends and wider circle of acquaintances gradually get drawn into seeing you as a figure of fun, and at work you've gone from being a cheerful workmate to someone the boss is keeping a watchful eye on...

So, where are you now? From someone once on a career path you've now become a lightweight, arguably insignificant figure, and now from that point it's not so hard to project forward to an ongoing consequence for any future job applications.

Improbable? Unlikely? Well, even allowing for artistic licence, the story's definitely not impossible by any stretch of the imagination. Consequences can take on a life of their own.

The philosopher and writer Rudolf Steiner, in lectures given in the years just before the First World War, took a radical view of consequences. He asserted that, as death takes over a person, their 'soul' makes a return journey, literally reversing through the course of their life, experiencing and understanding the events resulting from their actions, and the incidents/behaviours that led to those actions and reactions. Then, at the point of conception, a new life can take on the 'soul' of that departing life – obviously, in the process, benefitting from the wisdom and understanding of that return journey.[1]

Karma

The word 'karma' is variously defined as a law or principle that all actions – whether literally deeds, or simply words or even thoughts — have a reaction. Cause–consequence. Some might say 'what goes around comes around'.

There's every chance you think these types of ideas are *way* too deep. But they illustrate how keenly people have felt, not just over years or generations, but millennia, the significance of understanding consequences.

Understanding that, actually taking the time to appreciate *fully* that you are the architect of your own future, is crucially important in seeing the value of the PBT method. If you haven't seen the consequences of your actions before — because you've never given yourself time to visualize all the 'what ifs' in your life — you now have the perfect tool.

> *'Sometimes when I consider what tremendous consequences come from little things... I am tempted to think... there are no little things.'*
> **BRUCE BARTON**

We'll delve into consequences plenty more times before we're through. No surprise there — it's central to this technique. It is really the reason we developed the Pause Button system in the first place. To help you have those extra few moments to think; to give yourself breathing space, both figuratively and literally, to make your mind up about how you want your life to be *right now*, in the present. Taking your own time, knowing you don't *have* to do anything apart from think. Knowing that pressing Pause has provided a buffer against your craving, your rage, your anxiety, your fear, your compulsion — in fact, in many ways it provides you with a buffer against the world for as long as you need one. You're on freeze frame, in safe mode, in the PBT zone, and you get to do all the thinking necessary to make the right choice when you feel ready to move on.

You've very likely read this and thought, 'Yes, that sounds like a good idea.' Perhaps even bought this book on the basis of wanting help with your problem – with making the right choices at the right time.

But – and make no mistake, this is a big but – you not only need to sign up to the theory, you must also understand absolutely and completely what this means, and just how to think yourself through the process and come out ready to make a different choice on the other 'side' of the Pause.

To really, truly 'get it', you also need to 'get' the cause and effect of your decisions. To recognize the connection between the Fast Forward button and the ramifications of 'giving in' to your trigger. To STOP, SEE and FEEL in advance how you'll be feeling a bit further down the road.

So try it now. You're reading this book. Using your Pause Button card, or crooking your index finger and thumb, press Pause. It might well feel slightly silly the first time, or you might be so totally at home with remote controls, and so keen to make changes in your life, that you flow seamlessly into this new way of thinking. Maybe this time, and the next time or two, actually get a remote control in your hand. Remind yourself how your fingers work the control, virtually without the need to think about it. (And hold *that* thought, too… learning things so thoroughly they become unconscious actions is something we'll come to shortly!)

Right, you're on Pause. You now have that time to think. You're frozen; no one's going to *make* you drink that drink, *make* you shout at the kids, *make* you drive recklessly or *make* you behave in any of the myriad ways that may have led you, in the past, to despair that you'll ever change.

Martin's thoughts on consequences are clear. When we start to think about the consequences of our actions, everything changes — from how we deal with our overdraft and how we speak to our children, to our fear of the dentist. Every time we think about the results of our actions, everything can change in a heartbeat. We can take control. If we choose to.

Marion agrees, and impresses on people that it's all about the choices they make in a particular situation at a given time. You choose how you're going to behave, but you need to be aware of what's going to happen as a result of your behaviour, and be prepared to face the aftermath of your decision and take responsibility for your actions.

Of course, as we well know, sometimes there seems to be no choice. Tunnel vision kicks in, and all you seem able to think about is that trigger, the actions you're so used to doing. Marion's answer to that? It's about stopping yourself from having a knee-jerk reaction. About freezing the moment and giving yourself a chance to stand back and think, what do I *want* to happen?

You can't change what's happened in the past, but you can change how you're about to react in any given situation right now. You *can* change that. Yes, in the past you might have done something different and regretted it, but now you can decide to *change* your reaction — and as a result, you'll get different, much more positive and beneficial consequences that you're likely to feel much happier about.

'Knee-jerk reaction type responses are NOT actually chosen in the moment. While they do flow from us in the now, they were chosen in prior days, weeks, and months. The knee-jerk reaction is a type of response that is the result of a cumulative pattern of choices, decisions we've made in prior days that set-in-motion an automatic and "unthinking"

> *response that emerges in the now. Unthinking responses are termed... Reactions. Like a landmine ready to explode, knee-jerk reactions are waiting to explode at some future time as we are "stepped on".*
> **MATT MOODY PHD[2]**

It's a bit like cost–benefit analysis, if you understand that concept. What does your current problematic behaviour cost you? Not in monetary terms, of course – although with some issues, such as substance abuse, money is a factor – but in anxiety, stress, raised blood pressure, family disagreements, etc.? What would it 'cost' you to change your behaviour? The cost of this book? Some numbers of hours of practice? Now offset that against the benefits. The improvement in your bank balance. The improvement in your home life. Maybe improvements in your health, your career, your friendships. How does the cost analysis of change look now?

Or maybe you'd prefer to look at increasing, in your mind's eye, the size of the benefit of change and diminishing the size of the benefit of not changing? Try to put a value on how you feel about the way you are; the behaviour you exhibit, and what that means to you. Then, also put a value on how you'll be if you change. Then you can weigh up, compare and assess the relative importance of each of these to you.

The inability to choose a larger 'benefit' or 'pay-off' further into the future, in place of a smaller benefit right now, is called 'delay discounting' by psychologists.[3] If you can truly grasp the idea that you will be getting a far greater payback as a result of the passage of time, you have made a great advance in your learning. This is particularly relevant in the case of weight loss and management. Having spent a long time becoming overweight, many people then have severe problems accepting it will take a significant period of time to shed that excess weight. In the short term, they're not going to see a sudden change in their shape, or their clothes size, and it all seems so far into the future.

Weighing up how good it will feel when they achieve their goal weight and size is part and parcel of the cost–benefit value calculations. It amounts to avoiding 'delay discounting'!

Time perspective, a theory developed by Professor Philip Zimbardo, is simply explained as the measure by which people live their lives according to the importance they place on time – past, present and future – and the negative or positive focus they allocate to each one.[4]

You could be focused on the 'good old days', only interested in today, or prioritizing your future. All of these have relevance to *how* you choose to live your present-day life. Maybe you rein yourself in because of your over-emphasis on what happened the last time you did *x*, or keep yourself tightly under control on the basis that you have to plan constantly for the future. Perhaps you are really only interested 'in the moment', with not much thought given to next month or next year, or 10 years down the line.

(You can read more about these theories in Dr Theano Kalavana's contribution to this book in the Appendix.)

For example, what's the value of having fish and chips tonight? It's about specifying a number – say between 1 and 50. What's the value of the fish and chips? The batter? The salt and vinegar? Then see what value you'd put on dropping a size or two, not getting breathless when you play with the kids, not fearing your doctor's check-up in case you are further down the road to diabetes and clogged arteries. If the value you place on that healthier you is greater than the value of the fish and chips, you know your motivation.

The Change Equation

People will only change when the combination of the desire for change, the vision of the change, and the knowledge of the change process, is greater than the value of leaving things as they are. Dissatisfaction+vision+change process = the cost of change.

MANAGING COMPLEX CHANGE, BECKHARD AND HARRIS[5]

The tactic of thinking ahead, which is another way of describing what is suggested in PBT, is crucial to many things, some involving global consequences. Consider how vital it is for politicians and diplomats, for example, to look at all the possible results of their actions. To weigh up and take responsibility, not just for themselves, but for the actions suggested for their committees, their governments and how those play out in the international scene; what they might mean for entire populations. Maybe you are not the president of a country, nor even the president of a corporation, but even so there are plenty of situations where thinking ahead is vital.

Think of chess. Apart from professional players whose livelihoods depend on their ability, for most people chess is just a game. But many would argue it's the ultimate demonstration of a capacity to think ahead. A perfect embodiment of everything that is PBT. Pause (in some games of chess this is for a strictly limited period, so it reflects real life very accurately), Fast Forward (what if... I move my pawn there... she'll move her pawn there... or might she opt for the greater spatial movement of the knight?). Rewind. Fast Forward again (a whole different set of potential moves). Rewind. Make your decision and Play.

It's all about consequences – looking at them, understanding them and choosing what action you can take that will achieve the best result for you. Of course, you might be one of the many people who have always felt they haven't had a choice in the way things have happened. Someone or something else must be making the decisions, you think.

Well, PBT provides an answer to that. It gives you your control back. It's your life. You decide. To control your immediate thoughts and actions, which in turn control your life, all you really need to do is give yourself a little bit of 'frozen time'. Time to make more informed choices. Once learned (and it's really not all that difficult!) that technique will prove ground-breaking for many people. Your life will be back in *your* control!

Though it might seem a red herring, it is vital to understand that making (reaching, taking, whichever word you prefer!) a decision needn't mean some clear-cut, negative or positive, life-changing choice. In fact, even deciding *not* to decide is making a decision. Yes, read that again. If you are completely caught up in a complex family problem, or can't figure out the best thing to do about issues at work, or any choice at all, in fact, you may achieve more by effectively taking some mental time out. Let water pass under the bridge. Take the pressure off yourself. Just opt not to decide anything until some point in the future. Having made that choice, recognize that you *have* made a decision.

By putting off the more complicated decision, you *consciously choose* not to pressurize yourself any more than you can cope with right now.

Reckless Planning?

Let's take another sideways look at consequences. As well as recognizing that every action has a consequence, you need to learn as much as you possibly can about what you do (or don't do) to lead to them. You might like to consider the phrase 'Take responsibility for your actions'. After all, it's what your grandmother might have said, isn't it?!

Your understanding of consequences will eventually come to you. It may happen in a defining 'light bulb' moment, or it may be a gradual realization. Once you've recognized your part in everything that happens 'to' you, once you've sat up and thought, 'OK, life's not dealing me a bad hand; I'm involved in picking the cards myself', you're approaching another epiphany. There are those who would suggest we have to come to terms with the possibility that choosing consequences pretty much amounts to planning – or at least pre-planning. All the time, people are planning their days. Arranging their afternoons. Deciding what to do later in the evening. Maybe later in life!

We should make it clear here that we're not suggesting that the people who chose, for example, to be in Thailand during the 2004 tsunami could be said to have chosen the dire consequences they experienced. And those living on the poverty line invariably don't do it by choice. Those in a position to exercise choice are the ones we're targeting. Those with the foresight – and, unquestionably, choice – to buy this book would be prime examples!

You plan your actions, sometimes in minute detail. Have you ever considered that, by doing this, you're also effectively *planning* the consequences?[6] Sounds too obvious? It works both ways, though – good and bad. Those mistakes of the past may actually have resulted from a carefully organized sequence of events, set up by you and yet, by not stopping, pressing Pause and thinking through what would happen, you've short-changed yourself. Planned, just not thoroughly enough. Failed to 'see it through' in your mind's eye. Leading to what might sometimes be dire consequences.

That friendless adult we mentioned a while back? How about thinking of his bullying behaviour as a child in terms of planning. He planned his future by behaving that way. Maybe not the way he would have wanted things to turn out, but he planned it nonetheless. Turning the theory around might just have you taking a much, much closer look at your own behaviour. Did you *plan* for your children to avoid you in the evenings because that's when your temper is at its worst? Did you *plan* to alienate your children's friends' mothers by giving in to the impulse to make bitchy comments?

Obviously not, we hear you chorus! Yet think about it. If you'd pressed Pause, and considered, you probably would have behaved differently. You didn't choose to think of the consequences, so you could say that the lack of choice actually played a part in 'planning' these outcomes.

Have you ever heard someone say, 'This didn't go the way I planned'? Did you sympathize? Just stop for a moment and put the comment in the context of reckless planning. Of paying scant attention to our choices and their consequences. Might that person's life/career/holiday/marriage have been totally different if they'd been a bit more mindful of outcomes when making all the minute (and, no doubt, not so minute) judgements, decisions and choices along the way?

Didn't go the way she'd planned? Well, think about it a bit – what she didn't like was the consequences of her actions!

Let's take a look at a single definition of the word 'reckless' – a word that has the connotation of lack of care, not minding what might happen when you're about to do something. That one definition is, 'careless of consequences'.[7] If you interrupt that 'careless' process by pressing Pause, none of your actions after that moment can possibly be reckless. You will have had time to visualize the possible outcomes of whatever action(s) you were about to take. You'll have slowed down or stopped your actions, removing your own mental pressure for a decision, and interjecting the thing that's missing in the definition: Care, Thought, Deliberation.

Ever thought your behaviour was extemporaneous? Not unless your vocabulary includes that word, we're sure of that! One definition is 'composed, performed or uttered on the spur of the moment'.[8] An example being that lots of criminal behaviour is extemporaneous – i.e., happening suddenly and without clearly understood causes. In fact, it's the exact opposite of premeditated.

You really ought to spend a moment or two looking at the kind of synonyms available in the marvel that is the English language: unplanned, unpremeditated, offhand, snap, unrehearsed, casual, haphazard, hit-or-miss, ill-advised, impetuous, abrupt... All are the sign of decisions or actions done without PBT.

If you stop, press Pause and run through the consequences of your action mentally, can you see the difference in the range of words we could then use? Measured, reasoned, thoughtful, thought-out, purposefully, carefully, with foresight; given the richness of our language, the list actually goes on. And on!

It's as if by being irresponsible, *reckless*, not considering the consequences of your actions, you 'choose' your course of action, effectively building in, predicting, *planning*, the outcome.

Yet logic tells you that the choice, the planning, of an outcome is not possible. Wouldn't it be better to spend a few moments on Pause and change your present to be the way you'd prefer?

For example, by having an affair, allowing yourself the instant gratification of that sexual thrill, you may well threaten your marriage, your family's stability, your home life, your children's lives. Was your recklessness in conducting the affair a form of planning? By pressing Pause when you started to realize there was a bit of chemistry with that other person, would you have had sufficient time and space to imagine all the consequences and ultimately chosen different actions? And, of course, a different outcome?

Some academics will tell you that you cannot choose *both* action and consequence. They'll say you have a choice to do something, but that you then have to accept the consequences. Dr Steven R. Covey says, 'While we are free to choose our actions, we are not free to choose the consequences of our actions.'[9] We would respectfully disagree with him. You may not be able to guarantee any accuracy in predicting the consequences of your actions, but you can make a jolly good estimation/calculation. Allowing for a clear understanding of probability, we'd say you can (probably) predict the consequence of your actions. Which bears more than a passing resemblance to having a choice.

The trick is to understand which consequences come with which actions, and to make the right choice of action to achieve the preferable outcome for you.

So, in a situation in which you might believe you'll always repeat the mistakes you've made in the past, you can now draw a line and say, 'I'm interested in my present and my future now; I can't change the past but I can press Pause and change how I'm about to react in this situation right now – I can change that and get different consequences that are much more positive and beneficial, and which I'll feel happy about.'

Of course, further down the line you'll be in a better place to realize you can also choose consequences. For example, you can choose that you want to graduate with a good degree, ensuring a better chance of putting yourself on the career path you've long aspired to. So, with that consequence in mind, you can be pretty sure the likeliest way of achieving it is by not partying till dawn all year, by avoiding alcohol or substance abuse, and by generally working hard. Whether your ultimate choice of action gets you the consequence you've been wanting, well...

> *'Wisdom consists of the anticipation of consequences.'*
> **NORMAN COUSINS**

It's Not All About You

Students of karma would consider us remiss if we didn't also emphasize that, in looking at cause and effect, action and reaction, and consequences in general, you should also take account of making conscious decisions to do 'good' as well as conscious decisions not to do 'harm'.

Outside of the Pause Button moments, spend some time considering how it makes you feel when you have said, or done, something which is positively encouraging, entertaining or life-enhancing for those around you. When you smiled at a stranger in a bus queue. Picked up a dropped coin for someone in a supermarket. Blew a raspberry at a bored child, getting smiles not only from the child, but from the previously harassed parents.

Try to recall situations where you've brought joy to others by your actions or words. How did they feel? How did that make you feel? When your ageing grandmother got in touch to say how very much she appreciated that lovely letter you wrote, despite your rarely putting pen to paper these days? When your 20-something child sent a card thanking you for all your support when she moved house?

The answer to these questions is, of course, that you will have felt considerably more positive, not only about life, but about yourself. Taking that one step further, the logical progression is that it would be worth making the effort to focus specifically on acting in ways that bring joy or positivity to others. Both for the boost to yourself and for the happiness you'll create around you.

> *'One who smiles rather than rages is always the stronger.'*
> **JAPANESE PROVERB**

How does this relate to Pause Button Therapy? Well, just think of long-distance runners. How do they train? Clearly there's a mix, but actually marathon runners are taught to include a series of bursts of sprint speed within their training schedules. This is done because it is shown to increase their overall speed. Speed typists? Before taking an exam they've drilled and drilled and drilled, rattling off short exercises at extraordinary speeds to ensure success at the (slightly lower) grade they've been entered for. In other words, attempting to 'go the extra mile' to achieve positive outcomes — actually practising good karma, maybe — should give you the 'slack', almost the PBT-style breathing space, to visualize and fully understand the consequences of the more negative behaviours for which you think PBT may help.

If you've experienced the benefits of the other side of the coin – of proactive 'good' actions – logic would tell you it will be far easier to recognize the downsides that result when you opt for less positive behaviour.

If you didn't send that 'thank you' note to your granny, what would the consequences be? Would she feel slightly lonelier… not enough to complain, of course, but would her life be that bit duller? That stranger you smiled at passing the bus stop, would their day otherwise have been totally devoid of human communication? It's not so improbable in today's hurried world. If you've taken the trouble to accumulate the 'good karma', you're far better equipped to understand the flip side.

You might now be less surprised to read that overcoming your repetitive anger could easily have a second beneficial side effect. If you've used the Pause Button to think about the consequences of your actions, and are finding it easy to simply be less angry, the follow-on from that is that you can start to see positive actions to take, as opposed to solely negative actions to cut out. You press Pause to not overreact when your husband wants to change the soap channel to watch a football match. How about taking that a step further and considering how selfish you tend to be by watching 'your' programmes four nights a week. Maybe you'll now start to Pause and change to his channels without discussion or argument, half the time?

Maybe your child wants to go to the zoo and you've 'far better' things to do. In time, after pressing Pause, you'll find yourself thinking how much more quality time, and fun, you could have if you just went with what they want a bit more often.

There's another, slightly deeper reason for choosing the simple process of freezing time. Using the Pause Button technique stops the moment. You can then look at what you will feel if you act a certain way; how it will impact on those around you. You can then Rewind, Fast Forward, then Pause again to see the effects of a different course of action.

Or, and this is an additional benefit, you could just spend some extra time delving into your soul/heart/psyche to discover just why some of your behaviours play such a disproportionate part in your life. You could even take a closer look at the consequences of positive, life-affirming actions like the ones we touched on earlier. The teacher who complimented the behaviour of a child… and went on to compliment the parents for their skill in raising the child? How much more positive were those parents that day (and the next, and the next)?

If you allow yourself some extra 'me' time, some thinking space – but, in this case, outside the immediacy of decision-making – you might find yourself starting to see a pattern to your 'bad' behaviours. And, as we've said so many times, spotting that trigger moment so you can press Pause is absolutely fundamental. If you can sense the kinds of occasion that have been a problem for you in the past, you are far better placed to use your PBT knowledge in the future.

> **The Pause Button freezes time, allowing people to consider their actions and to change how they feel or what they may do. We feel it can be taken further: people learning to Pause their mind will gain a clearer insight into why certain behaviours are part of their lives.**

Of course, as with all therapy, there's no guarantee that the introduction of any of these things will happen to any major degree overnight. The changes you're seeking? They might not appear to be as dramatic or as immediate as you were hoping. Maybe you need to understand yourself in a little more depth to be able to master the skill of living more successfully in the present. Using PBT to understand why you act the way you do, how you cope, why you feel a certain way, could benefit you as much as being able to stop yourself from continually making rash decisions.

As part of that process you will inevitably spend some time analyzing how you've reacted in the past. Here's an extreme but totally plausible example:

A guy drives home in his brand new, shiny and somewhat expensive car. He's saved all his bonuses for three years, his night shift money, the sly betting wins. He's enjoying the smell of the showroom-shiny interior. He's so proud and he's itching to show his wife. Not far to go now. He pulls up at the lights, smiles at himself in the rearview mirror. God, what a brilliant day. Smack. A car comes up behind and smashes into his bumper. No chance to get out and challenge the culprit; he's overtaken as the lights change and shoots off ahead. Our man catches up with him at the next red light and blocks him in from behind so he can't go anywhere. The red mist is gathering. He gets out of the car, knocks on the window, ready to shout, yell, bawl, maybe even smack him. Red in the face, forehead veins up, heart thumping. Heading for a heart attack. He knocks on the window again. The little guy inside winds down the window, sobbing uncontrollably. He passes out a £50 note, saying, 'I'm sorry. Take it, it's all I've got, here's my number. My son's on a life support in the hospital up the road, they've just called. I've got 10 minutes to get there and say goodbye. I'm sorry.'

Now how does he feel? He completely misread the situation. Assumed it was just another careless driver. He didn't give a moment's thought, not the slightest, to an alternative scenario.

He realized too late he'd reacted completely wrongly, and not thought about the possible consequences of what he was about to do. Or what might be happening in anyone else's life.

How many of us have done this? Perhaps not exactly this, but something similar. Something hasty and ill-judged? Put your hands up.

Realistically, you've probably already started analyzing the actions and reactions that have had such an impact on your life so far. Without that soul-searching, it's likely you wouldn't have established that you need to make changes. Recognizing how the past has influenced your behaviour, your reactions and, therefore, effectively influenced your life as it is now, can provide some comfort and help you to work through to a fuller understanding of your fears, failings, hopes and dreams. Leaving you with the tools to make today that much better.

How Hollywood Sees It

Movie makers have hit upon the understanding of cause and effect in many different ways. Some well-known examples are:

The Ashton Kutcher film *The Butterfly Effect*, which turns the idea slightly on its head by suggesting that the main character, through reading his diary of past events, can 'tweak' his actual present-day life.

Sliding Doors took a moment in time – the character only just squeezing into a departing underground train – and then looked at the events that occurred after she got on the train and then also if she hadn't made it.

Crash told how the lives of a group of strangers were actually going to become linked in ways they could never have predicted, just because of actions, reactions and consequences.

Even *Sleepless in Seattle* touches on this notion, when, at the end, the two main characters just miss each other by their choice of elevator to the top of the Empire State Building.

Just as much about consequences, though from a different perspective, is the scene in the much-loved Julia Roberts/ Richard Gere rom-com *Pretty Woman* when, having been turned down as a customer simply because of her somewhat (how shall we put this?) trashy appearance, Julia Roberts' character, Vivian, returns to a Rodeo Drive fashion store wearing some of her new, and very, *very* expensive clothes. She challenges the assistant who snubbed her: 'Do you remember me?' She gets the salesperson to admit they work on commission, and then hits her with the memorable line: 'Big mistake. Big. Huge!'

Amusing, maybe, but if the staff had had their Pause Button minds in focus on the day of her first visit, they'd have thought about the consequences of serving her – potential sales, commission, recommendation to friends, compliments from Vivian's acquaintances and further sales, etc. And the alternative consequence? The one playing out in front of them. She *did* have the money they assumed she didn't. In fact, she had copious amounts of cash to spend just on clothes. By turning her away, they threw all those commission/sales/possibilities in the trash, and also potentially endangered their jobs.

Ripple Effect

Martin Shirran has described consequences as nothing more nor less than a 'ripple effect'. This is also the title of Forest

Whitaker's 2007 movie in which his fashion designer character is about to make it big when he has a marital/business crisis. He feels this may be bad karma for something he did 15 years previously, and tries to put right the wrong. Does this sound a bit like what we've been talking about?

...And Now for the Weather Forecast

Weather systems may seem totally irrelevant to a discussion about consequences; however, not only are weather forecasts actually a perfect example of how you can attempt to predict the outcome of a series of actions (if the pressure drops, x will happen, if the temperature rises, y will happen, if they both occur, z will happen), but if you mix both philosophy *and* meteorology, you reach the Butterfly Effect, which is a part of chaos theory.

Edward Norton Lorenz originally worked with the possibility that the wind generated by seagulls' wing movements could cause a change in the weather.[10] The seagulls example got changed to butterflies, but the principle is the same. Could a minute action actually cause a major change to something else, somewhere else? And if Lorenz's thoughts are applied to human behaviour, seemingly insignificant decisions, actions and comments may ultimately have unexpectedly greater consequences.

Actions you and others have taken in reality, in the here and now, and even actions and experiences stored in the unconscious mind, could play a part in affecting a person's behaviour in equally unpredictable and unexpected ways. A kind of double whammy. Actions you and others have taken, and also actions you barely even remember, could make imperceptible changes to how you think and, therefore, to how you act/react. Think about the massive consequences of the First and Second World Wars. The millions of lives lost, and the effects on the lives of families for generations. The historical facts – everything that happened, even information read after the fact by people too young to have experienced the war themselves – will affect perceptions and, in turn, affect actions and reactions.

One sad illustration of this phenomenon is teen suicide, where there's been no obvious previous depression. Families can spend years just analyzing and re-analyzing all the tiniest possible factors that may have triggered the suicide.

All of which may seem worlds away from Pause Button Therapy. But has it made you think about cause and effect? The 'what ifs' of life? In fact, taking a magnifying glass to these is central to what this chapter is all about: emphasizing the importance of understanding that every single thing you say or do has consequences.

With PBT you now have the tools to stop and consider which set of consequences you prefer and, therefore, which action to take!

'I want to be a jerk like the rest of my friends,
and have fun, and not care about the consequences,
but I just can't now.'
LEONARDO DiCAPRIO

A PAUSE BUTTON MOMENT

Since his marriage broke down, David had become more and more depressed. He found he was constantly tired, and became involved in fewer and fewer social events. He thought there was nothing positive in his future; at times he wondered if there was any point in going on. Concerned about him, his sister convinced him to see a counsellor, and one of the interventions used was PBT.

By using the Fast Forward and Rewind buttons, David was able to see how his negative thoughts were often inappropriate. He was encouraged to see that a thought is just that, and learned to press Fast Forward to see the much more positive consequences if he behaved, thought, reacted differently. PBT is not always going to be a quick process, and in David's case it took quite some time, but ultimately, by using his Fast Forward and Rewind enough times, he was able to make better choices most of the time.

IN THIS CHAPTER, YOU'VE LEARNED:

- You might actually be planning, but recklessly.
- Do your actions affect your loved ones?
- Visualizing consequences.

*Pause * Think * Decide * Act*

5

IF ONLY... THE SALUTARY TALE OF ONE MAN'S BAD CHOICES

'Though no one can go back and make a brand new start, anyone can start from now and make a brand new ending.'

CARL BARD

The following is not fiction. It is the story of the life (so far) of one young British man. Over several hours in a face-to-face interview, he laid bare the mistakes, crimes and poor judgements, as well as other people's often equally bad choices, that moulded his development from a happy child to a career criminal.

Yet of course it could all have been so different. Once you've read a flavour of his reality, we'll take you through an imaginary *Sliding Doors* scenario in which he has the opportunity to take advantage of those few moments Paused – using PBT – to consider the consequences and alter his could-have-been course of action.

But first, here's what really happened:

As a boy, Graham Hodges dreamed the same dreams as most kids brought up near the windswept sands of his home town of Great Yarmouth in Norfolk. Football, sandcastles, bikes, all the stuff you'd expect. But being a fireman was his main dream.

Talk to him today, though, and it's a different person you'll meet. Not a fireman, but a man in his late twenties still unable to do more than draw Jobseeker's Allowance for the unemployed. A man whose life has been all but completely destroyed by a series of events and decisions he now regrets so much he can barely describe them. 'If I could go back in time I would change everything,' he says.

Well, maybe not everything. Saving a man's life in a dangerous river rescue at the tender age of 15. Receiving a Certificate of Commendation from the police for his bravery. Meeting the Queen at Sandringham House as a result. He's justly proud of those. And incredibly proud of turning around from a life of crime that's seen him jailed twice and holding a criminal record some 15 pages long. That's the life he's far from proud of; the life that still has such a negative effect that it's holding him back from the future he so desperately craves.

He's moved on so very far from the serial offender of his teens and the 20 car thefts and 16 burglaries. Now he can clearly see his poor choices. What's more, he now knows he could have avoided some or maybe all the decisions that led to his disastrous career in crime – by using PBT.

We spoke to Graham to get a picture of his life to date, and an idea of how he now recognizes things might have panned out differently. His is a story of mischief and crime and, underlying it all, a hefty dose of family tragedy. He is not the only man whose adulthood has been shaped by things he couldn't control as a child. Nor the only one to have allowed himself to be swayed into doing things because he just didn't stop and think about the consequences.

It's a long story; and, you might think, not a special one. Why bother reading it? Because it's also a story with echoes of the kinds of bad decisions we might all make.

Who reading this now can honestly say they haven't had at least a dozen 'I wish I hadn't...' or 'Why didn't I...?' or 'What if...?' or 'If only...' moments in the past *month*, never mind the past 15 years? And in Graham's story, not all the poor choices were his. Later on we'll take a second look at the tale – but with a PBT slant.

Graham lost his mum when she died from a brain tumour. He was just seven years old. 'It was heartbreaking for me growing up without her, but also watching my friends being picked up from school by *their* mums,' he says. This was on top of rarely seeing his dad, who had left when Graham was tiny.

Though now, in his mid-twenties, he has scant memory of his mum without help from photographs, Graham remembers one thing – a hazy, warm, loving image. He was scared of the dark as a small boy, and if he woke up in the middle of the night, he would creep into bed with his mum for comfort. 'We were really close, I know that,' he says.

His mum's dying wish was for her small boy to live with his elder sister or maternal grandmother. One of Graham's sisters was awarded custody of him, but his new life did not provide calm security.

He knows that losing his mum, and not seeing his dad, left him without a parent to teach him right from wrong. His schooling was affected, too – and not just by way of poor grades. He got into trouble for acting up when people said mean things like, 'At least I've got a mum.' People would wind him up, and often he reacted very badly, sometimes being removed from class and isolated as a result.

Almost predictably, the step into crime seems to have happened seamlessly for Graham. 'My first crime was when I was about 12', he explains. 'I was with a friend and we were bored. We managed to get into a warehouse and saw tins of paint, so threw it around everywhere. We also stole a chainsaw. That was just stupid.

'I don't know why I thought it was OK to do it', he continues. 'We had been throwing stones in the water and we looked in an open window.

'Our families called the police, thinking we might get a reward because we told them we'd found the chainsaw in a bush, and they had believed us. However, small footprints had been found in paint at the warehouse, and when the police came around my trainers were covered in paint...' The lads ended up receiving a caution and having to write a letter to the warehouse owner and apologize in person.

Within two years, alcohol was playing a part. 'The family used to have a drink together on a Friday night to socialize,' Graham says. 'To start with I'd just say yes to a drink, to be sociable. But then it got out of control a little bit.'

At school, hanging around with a friend, Graham was offered marijuana and said he'd give it a go. He remembers someone saying that, if you do it long enough, you'll want something stronger. At about 15 he started taking Ecstasy, sometimes ending up being rushed to hospital after having a fit.

He was not, by any means, a career criminal when he became involved in a daring river rescue. This turned out to be a pivotal event, leading to a visit to the Queen's country residence at Sandringham in Norfolk, meeting the Queen and the Duke of Edinburgh – probably the proudest moment of Graham's life so far.

'I was with a friend. We'd just been to a youth disco night and were walking across the bridge over the river in Yarmouth when we heard a shout. We looked but couldn't see anything, then heard a louder shout for help. We looked down and saw a man in the water.

'My friend couldn't swim, but we couldn't just leave him there. There were lots of people nearby, but no one did anything. This guy was just holding on to a cable. I looked at the current and thought I'd be swept away. I jumped in, got hold of the man and held on to the cable, then used all my strength to get him onto the steps. This guy was huge – really big. I'm small now but then I was even smaller; I don't know how I did it. I managed to push him up the steps and then an off-duty paramedic ran over to help. When the police came they took my name, told me "well done" and gave me a lift home.'

Despite his efforts in one of the more dangerous river currents in the country, neither Graham nor his friend ever heard even a thank you from the man they had helped to save. 'A month or so later I received a letter informing me that I was to receive a bravery award from the Norfolk Constabulary.

'My friend got one as well, and it made us very popular with the girls! Then I received an invitation to a garden party at Sandringham; I remember my nan being so proud.

'It was the best time of my life, going there. It was amazing to be there, a foot away from the Queen, to shake the Duke of Edinburgh's hand. Until the day she died, Nan kept that invitation.'

Graham's criminal career started to spiral when his sister moved house and he began hanging around with a group he readily admits were 'the wrong people'. 'We used to go to big out-of-town supermarkets and [a girlfriend's mum] would steal a trolley full of alcohol and put it in the car and I'd drive away.'

The group he'd begun to associate with became more and more well known to police.

'We started stealing cars one night; we'd taken cocaine as well as being drunk,' says Graham. 'We walked past a car, saw a phone and smashed the window to take it, then ended up stealing it and driving round for a while... at the time [we] thought it was great. We carried on every night joyriding.'

The need for money for more drugs to share with the group led to the first burglary. 'Over the following year or so we stole many cars and burgled quite a few houses. It just escalated from there, really – more burglaries and getting into trouble with fights.

'Being drunk, someone would say something stupid and sometimes it would end up with us all being arrested for fighting with each other.'

He and a friend, both drunk, went out one night in his friend's mum's car. The friend lost control and swerved, hitting a kerb and facing oncoming traffic on Norfolk's notorious death-trap road 'the Acle Straight'. Within minutes they were speeding around a sharp bend, where his friend lost control again, hit the corner and the car bounced out of a ditch, finally ending up hitting a tree.

'A branch had come through the side window, trapping me by my legs. It took hours to be cut out, but it was a lucky escape because the tree could easily have taken my legs off.

'Eventually, it all caught up with me and I was sent to a Young Offender Institution,' Graham says. 'Not long after I arrived, I got into a fight with a man who said something about my mum. He threatened me, and as I came out of my cell, he slashed me with two razor blades, exposing the muscle and leaving a six-inch scar on my arm. I remember being taken to hospital in handcuffs. Of course, I couldn't tell them who'd done it, so they moved me to a different wing. I served the rest of my seven months, then went to Crown Court for trial.'

Warned by his barrister that he was likely to be looking at four to six years in prison, Graham said his goodbyes to his family. Surprisingly, however, the judge gave him a second chance and freed him.

'I remember I just stood there,' says Graham. 'A reporter and everyone in there just seemed to be shaking their heads in fury. Afterwards, at home, I remember sitting with my family indoors watching the news and my picture came up – "18-year-old Graham Hodges from Great Yarmouth was freed from court…" Then the victims, and people saying about all the old folk they said we'd burgled – and I thought, "Oh god". If anyone had robbed my nan's house I'd be so angry.'

Unfortunately, Graham didn't grab that second chance: 'I was still hanging around with the old crowd, and within another six months or so I committed another burglary and another car theft. I was on an electronic tag at the time [described as the last chance before a prison sentence] and [when I didn't turn up indoors at the right time], I was arrested again.'

This time, Graham decided to come clean about everything he'd done. His interview took some four hours, and shocked the policeman involved. 'I had to go through every detail, all the walk-ins at houses; everything. The only thing I didn't say was who else was involved, because it would have caused me big problems when I got out of jail.'

In court he was given a 10-month prison sentence – 'A lot better than the four years I was looking at the previous time,' says Graham. During this second stretch in Norwich Young Offender Institution, he decided to turn his life around. 'While I was in there my nan's partner, who I was quite close to, died. But because he wasn't a blood relative I wasn't allowed to go to the funeral. It made me think that next time it could be my nan. She was like my mum, really – we were so close.

'I sat there and really thought about what I was doing and the people I was hurting around me. Probably now I can see that a lot clearer, but yes, I did think then. You don't really get to do anything else but think when you're inside.

'When I came out of jail I had to get myself out of the road I lived in because that's where everyone lived that I used to hang around with,' Graham explains. 'So I moved in with my other sister. Moving was easy, but the hardest thing was to ditch all my friends. We'd been hanging around together for years. But I ditched everyone. I didn't go out of the house, didn't have any contact. To this day I still don't have contact with any of them. One of them I believe is in jail for armed robbery – and another's just got out of jail where he did four years for street robbery.'

Not that turning over a new leaf has been hassle-free. 'When I stopped getting into trouble,' says Graham, 'I would just be walking down the street and the police would come up and ask to search me.'

Naturally, Graham needed to find a job. Having studied welding in college, taken construction site safety training and also admin/IT training, he was doing all the right things – except it became obvious the criminal record was always in the way. Most employers checked what type of convictions he had, and that was the end of that.

Graham's record, incidentally, also shows some 2,000 hours of community service, a number of fines, disqualification from driving, probation – and that's not a complete list.

'I have stayed out of any trouble for such a long time, and surely people do deserve second chances, don't they? But it hangs over me, feels like it will for the rest of my life.

'I've applied to the Marines, too – they said try the Army; *they* said try the Air Force; *they* said try the Navy. In the end I gave up. I've gone for dozens of jobs – labouring, trainee butcher... It's a shame because I want it so much. But even though I'm the one that's suffering, I know it's all down to me. I've made a lot of wrong choices.'

Graham used to undertake caring for his nan in her later years, so he also thought of applying to become a carer, but again his path was blocked by his record. More recently he considered training for counselling, since he figures that to be a good counsellor you need to have been through things; however, he would probably need better GCSE qualifications.

Since leaving prison, in fact, Graham's only had one job, which took him 18 months to achieve. His uncle suggested a job as a lifeguard, because he is a good swimmer, and his nan paid for him to do the National Pools Lifeguard Qualification. A holiday park owner gave him a chance – Graham took his criminal record to the interview, but was told he didn't need it because they would do a check.

'I told him I'd kept myself out of trouble, not hanging around with the crowd I used to. Then, like now, all I wanted was for someone to give me a chance and prove to them that I'm good enough. So he gave me a chance.'

Graham then applied for another life-guarding job nearer home and was offered the position. He told his boss he'd got the new job, but then, on the day he was due to start, the new employer contacted him to say they couldn't let him take up the position because it involved handling money and his burglary convictions had shown up on the Criminal Records Bureau check. 'When I rang my old boss he told me they'd already taken someone else on. I just wish I'd never gone for the other job, because I'd probably still have been a lifeguard,' he says ruefully.

'It's a lot to take in. Sometimes I get really upset about everything that's happened in my life and just think it's not fair... But then I think, well, you've got to move on and try to live your life. But my record's in the way, stopping me from doing things.'

Some eight years after leaving prison, Graham lost the one person whom he had promised he would go straight. 'When Nan died it was heartbreaking,' he says. 'She was the one person I could sit down and say anything to. She was 91 and had lost a lot of mobility, but she was like a mum to me. For about a week after she died I had nightmares.

'If I'd lost her when I was in jail, it would have been awful. I just wanted her to be proud. That's when I decided enough was enough. I promised her I would do it. A lot of people said I wouldn't change my ways, but I've proved them all wrong. I've done it. And yes, she *was* proud of me.'

Graham has blotted his copybook since leaving jail, after about six years. 'I've seen plenty of police officers in the street who say I've done so well getting myself out of the situation I was in — but a fight broke out when I was at a nightclub with a friend. He was being hit by about three people and I tried to break it up, but got hit myself and retaliated. The police arrived and we got arrested. I was done for ABH [assault occasioning Actual Bodily Harm].

'I could have avoided that fight. I shouldn't have got involved. I know I should have just left it. I didn't go over to cause trouble. I was trying to split it up. If I'd paused and thought about the situation…'

'A few times in my life I've ended up quite depressed because I sometimes think it's quite unfair the way my life's turned out. I want to try to make something of my life now, get out there and do something.' He adds stoically, 'I'm 26 – still young enough to turn it all around. I've changed my life quite massively already.'

Makes you wonder, doesn't it? How much different *could* Graham's life have been? Really?

So, take a Pause of your own for a moment. Reconsider the question just asked. How could Graham's life have taken a different course? How many chances were there to alter the future?

If you have read the whole of his story you'll almost certainly have recognized some major 'if only' moments, some definite 'why did I do thats' and possibly some 'I wish I hadn't…' spots.

But if you look beneath the surface there are potentially hundreds, maybe even thousands, of times in Graham's life when he – and also often the people around him – might have made different choices which would have contributed to a whole different childhood/young adulthood, and now to a whole different life.

We are able to tell the story because Graham actually visited the Elite Clinics in Spain to undergo Pause Button Therapy. Now he is keen to help others by showing how very different his life, which started as such an ordinary life, would have been if he'd received this training years earlier.

Time to use the *Sliding Doors* scenario on some key parts of Graham's life, and see how things could have been so different now if Pause Button had been in the mix.

Let's Tell You About Graham #2...

The trauma of losing his mum obviously affected young Graham, but luckily, social workers and school staff, trained in PBT, were able to help him deal with his anxiety-induced rages. He had a few run-ins with authority, but was always helped back on track. Even today he says how much it helped, knowing the adults around him were using the same technique as he'd been taught. He missed some time at school, but achieved several decent grades at GCSE.

Graham is now a fireman of several years' standing and has been on many training courses to improve his career prospects. These have included special road accident rescue training and river/marine safety. He's a very popular member of the team and has many friends he socializes with on a regular basis.

He and his crew recently received an award for a brave rescue at an industrial estate in the town, and he had to attend a reception with local council dignitaries.

Several lads on his shift have got together to help run an after-school and weekend club for young people in his home town; the police support the venture and help with fundraising because it is such a positive move in a town with high youth crime problems.

Graham is married to Susan, who was a single mum with a toddler when they met — so he has a ready-made family. They're considering the possibility of Graham legally adopting five-year-old Luke. Graham takes great pride in taking Luke to the park to kick a football around.

They enjoy days on the beach, and Graham is pleased to have been able to teach Luke to swim at the local indoor pool.

He passed his driving test first time and, like many young men, enjoys taking his family into the countryside for picnics.

Graham and Susan are both working and have managed to save up a deposit to buy a flat on Great Yarmouth's seafront. With their spare cash they are able to afford annual visits to Graham's uncle in Spain. Graham did Spanish GCSE at school, which helps!

In a frame on the wall of the hallway of his flat are the invitation to the Sandringham garden party and the Norfolk Police Certificate of Commendation — both of which he's very proud of.

Graham was excited to have been accepted as a volunteer steward at the 2012 London Olympics.

Graham's dreams and aspirations for the future include possibly moving away from Great Yarmouth when Luke is a little older; he has always dreamed of living in Spain.

Of course, no one can say for sure what the future holds for any of us, but at the moment, for Graham the future looks bright. He still has fond memories of his mum, and of course, his nan. Clearly he wishes things could have been different, but he feels he's done the best he could with the cards he's been dealt in life.

Now let's have a look at some pivotal moments in Graham's (real) life and see how the consequences may have been different if Pause Button had been an option for him then.

What If... the Sister

How might things have been different for Graham if, when his mum died, the advice of professionals within Social Services had been sought? Maybe his sister getting custody was the right thing to happen for Graham, but she could/should have been offered support and guidance. Maybe she or another family member could/should have recognized she wasn't coping very well – that Graham was being allowed to 'get away with' mischief. What if someone had just paused for a few moments and thought about the consequences at all those points? Looked into the future on Fast Forward and spotted the tell-tale signs of trouble in the making? What if someone had looked into the future and seen how much the input of professional assistance would have altered young Graham's life for the better?

No child is ever 100 per cent perfectly behaved – Graham would still possibly have got into mischief, as most youngsters do to varying degrees, but maybe with parental/professional guidance it would have been nipped in the bud.

What If... School

What if one of Graham's teachers had used Pause Button Therapy when he was missing his mum so badly; maybe they'd have seen he needed extra help. Maybe they could/should have called in a counsellor far sooner and maybe he could/ should have been helped with his grieving process. Could someone have Paused and identified that he was effectively being bullied? Looked ahead to see the consequences with or without help.

What If... Drugs and Alcohol

What if drugs and alcohol had not played their part? Like most youngsters growing up in the UK, and many other Western countries – especially if they no longer have their parents around them – Graham may well have experimented with drugs and alcohol, but if he'd pressed Pause he could have looked at the consequences. Looked at how easy it would be to progress from marijuana to cocaine, and how having access to dealers would make Ecstasy just another step along the road to addiction. Even today he still enjoys going out for a few beers with his friends, but knowing the consequences of excess drinking makes it easier to choose to limit his intake.

What If...Crime

What if Graham's involvement in crime, other than normal schoolboy misdemeanours, had been limited to accepting a lift in a stolen car? Maybe if he had paid attention to lessons at school about the consequences of crime, he'd have stopped after that one time. Maybe if he'd been taught more about 'right and wrong' he would never have got in the car in the first place.

It's simple to see how, with just a few changes – stopping to think a few times in his formative years – Graham's life would have been different. How life for the victims of his crimes would have been different. How the cost to the taxpayer would have been different.

Starting to think of the consequences – how things could happen in the future – could have helped deliver Graham to the fairytale ending experienced by 'Graham #2'.

A PAUSE BUTTON MOMENT

Using PBT has helped Liam tackle his terrible road rage. Driving recklessly, in his mind at least, started out as fun, but after a while he got more and more angry at people who 'got in his way' on the roads. He liked to be first away from the lights, fastest round the bends, last to brake.

It wasn't long before he started having minor accidents. Once, a terrified driver reported him to the police for 'tailgating' his car for several miles after a dust-up at a junction. It was spiralling out of control. Points on his licence had led to increased insurance premiums. His family chose not to get in his car – it was too much of a risk.

One day his solicitor mentioned PBT, and how it could help so-called 'hot-headed' people like Liam. She'd even found him a counsellor keen to help.

At the very first session, Liam completely understood the principle. Now it was just up to him to press Pause if he felt that red mist rising when behind the wheel. And sure enough, as he drove to work the following morning and got stuck behind an elderly lady in her car, he figured he'd got nothing to lose. Swiftly pressing Pause, Liam looked at the two alternative consequences of his actions. If he overtook, hooting loudly, he stood a good chance of terrifying the lady, making her lose control and run off the road. She was about the same age as his granny – what would he think if some silly fool did that to her? The least that could happen would be he'd narrowly avoid a collision himself as he careered past her... just outside the school he went to as a child, where youngsters were running along the pavements. What would happen if, instead of a collision with a car, it was with a six-year-old? Just like his nephew?

So Liam pressed Rewind, then Fast Forward again to see the other choice. Take it slow for a few minutes, be a careful driver. It would only lose him maybe a minute or two. Wouldn't he be glad not to wear out his tyres faster than he needed to? Use up less fuel? And not endanger the life of someone his granny might know?

Liam pressed Rewind again, made a decision and got on with a better day, knowing he'd thought before acting.

IN THIS CHAPTER, YOU'VE LEARNED:

- So many 'what ifs'.
- Do you have fewer?
- Visualizing consequences.

*Pause * Think * Decide * Act*

6

21 DAYS TO CHANGE YOUR LIFE

'Watch your thoughts, for they become words.
Watch your words, for they become actions.
Watch your actions, for they become habits.'
ANONYMOUS

One of the most important lessons to learn in life, whether to do with PBT or not, is understanding that everything has a consequence. Yes, you've already read that – in previous chapters. Several times, if you were concentrating! Emphasizing that message is something we're likely to repeat quite a lot. Consequences, understanding they are inevitable, understanding your part in them and realizing *you* have it within you to begin to change the consequences you've been struggling with, is only one part of the story, though. A critical part, because without truly 'getting' that, you won't really – if you're honest with yourself deep down – see the need to take the next step. If you have any doubts whatsoever you should turn back to Chapter 4 and re-read what consequences are and how you're responsible for creating consequences by your actions. Then, and maybe only possibly then, will you be ready to move on.

So. That next step... *and, sorry, it's but actually more difficult than accepting that there are consequences...* is being totally ready to take action to prevent the consequences you *don't* want. If you can truly say you're ready to change, then maybe the time is right.

You know – you just *know* – you shouldn't have yelled at your kids. You are thoroughly ashamed of the way you behaved after you had that fourth vodka. You're cringing reading this, remembering the bad-mouthing you gave – *obviously* at full volume with expletives not deleted – right there, in full view of your kids, to that moron who cut you up as you pulled into a roundabout. More examples you can provide for yourself. You know what they are.

So, how do you get to intervene and make a different choice *before* your own thought processes get there a nanosecond ahead of you and take over? Obviously, we're saying you press Pause. But how do you get pressing Pause to be instinctive? How do you slot that Pause Button moment in *before* you've done whatever it is you'd rather you'd given yourself time to reconsider?

It's easy to explain, easy to do – but only if you're good and ready. Are you a driver? Did you learn to knit as a child? Can you ride a bike? Tie shoelaces? Swim? All of these things, even if you've not done them for years, you'd pick up again with barely a second thought. Because they're things you've learned to do to the extent that you don't need to be shown again.

It's not the same as breathing, as that's a physiological part of being a living creature. Nor like a heartbeat. Obviously. Yet habits can become almost instinctive. They can seem so much more a part of you than what they are – which is a variety of learned behaviours. That's if they're repeated often enough. Instinct is the level you need to aim at when creating a new habit: in this case, the habit you want to develop is using your Pause Button.

Given that researchers can find direct links, and calculate the speed of reaction of the smile or frown muscle groups in the face when people are shown 'happy' or 'angry' or 'negative' visual stimuli, you can see just how instantaneous some of our responses are.[1]

In experiments done in Sweden, the subjects believed they were being checked for sweat gland activity, so they had no idea their facial muscle activity was the real subject of the work. In fact, their only instruction was to look at different pictures, yet they reacted spontaneously and without effort.

A driver put behind the wheel will, apparently without a moment's thought, be using all four limbs, both eyes, both ears and various parts of their brain. Yet they will still be able to have a conversation, consider where they're going, and adjust various important and less important controls of the car, barely even aware they're doing it.

'The chains of habit are generally too small to be felt until they are too strong to be broken.'
SAMUEL JOHNSON

Essentially, you need PBT to be like this. Use it and use it until it becomes seemingly instinctive. We say 'seemingly', because there are countless academics who've spent years defining the distinction between habit and instinct. This goes back to one Charles Darwin, who really fanned the flames of debate when he suggested that some instincts grew from lifetime habits and could be passed through generations – a distinctly flawed theory; over a hundred years later, there is still fierce debate and much research into whether, for example, a bodybuilder can hand their strength genetically to their child.[2]

Theories now suggest though that the capacity to acquire an instinct might be inherited to such an extent that it appears so inbuilt as to be instinctive.[3] Even if you don't hope to pass your ability to 'learn' a habit to your children, you do need to address, here and now, how to acquire a habit for yourself – the simple habit of stopping and thinking before each and every action, each and every word you say, every last little thing you do. As we said before, without developing the ability to recognize that almost imperceptible moment when a thought prompts, then becomes, an action, you aren't even partway to being able to step in and create your Pause Button instinct.

So how did you get so accustomed to driving? Once upon a time it was a bogeyman in your head – at learner driver stage, we bet you thought you'd never even be able to master clutch control, parallel parking or mirror-signal-manoeuvre, let alone doing all those and more! What happened to change that to something so easy-peasy-lemon-squeezy? You did it. And did it again. And once more. And dozens of times. Hundreds. That's how it got to be automatic. And that's what you need.

A gifted child may only need to do something once or twice to be able to understand the concept and repeat it in the future. Normal children might need a dozen repetitions. Some language experts say you need to use a word 10 or more times to fully grasp it and add it to your vocabulary.[4]

The same principle applies to learned behaviour, habits, habitual responses, or whichever label you prefer to use. Psychologists and therapists work on a scale of approximately 18 to 30 days to 'create' a habit. So if you want to implant a

'Pause Button' that you don't even have to call upon or think about, it's up to you.

> *'I think things become habits when we get the pay-offs that we want. So if you get a pay-off from a behaviour, that can become habitual.'*
> **GAY JONES**

Where to start? Well, consequences arise from actions (and, logically, from reactions, too) – and those actions and reactions are, however subconscious you may feel they are, actually choices. Flag up to yourself when you might need to make a choice, and you've taken the first step.

Some choices, of course, are so seemingly minor you're possibly shouting out 'irrelevant' or 'trivial' or 'You're kidding, right?' Well no, sorry, we're not.

Before you get in the car to go to work, stop and think. Did I say goodbye to my family nicely? Have I forgotten anything? Did I leave the house reasonably tidy? Will I need to refuel the car before I get to work? On the way home? Should I put a raincoat in the car? Do I know my family's schedule for the day? What would the consequences be for me, or anyone else, if I do those things, or if I don't do any of them?

You'll be forgiven for thinking this really is over-repeated irrelevance. The kind of things you think about every day. Maybe, maybe not.

If you think about these things on a daily basis, it's probably in a cursory way, not necessarily following through to the alternate outcomes if you do or don't do something.

Seeing, feeling and experiencing the consequences of your actions. To get on the Pause Button road, though, it's vital to recognize consequences – and that's why it's important to start talking yourself through every last little detail of every choice you make. And don't try excusing yourself from this process because it's going to take so long. Go back to the earlier paragraph. Each of those questions, even followed through to the two 'what ifs', need only take an absolute maximum of about 10 to 15 seconds. Using those 15 seconds to figure out which is the best option for you and those around you – is that a waste of time?

So, extend this to the drive to work. Those junctions coming up where you usually just sail straight through, confident of your own ability – how about asking yourself 'what if' a learner driver is coming around the blind bend, not yet at ease with the controls? What would the consequences be for you, your day, your family, if you took a few seconds longer (not only thinking about your choice but all the ramifications, the other people affected by the consequences) and waited to get clear visibility? What would the outcome be if you cut your speed going past the school because you'd made a conscious choice to leave yourself more travel time? Would you avoid hitting the child who was about to step into the road because their parent had their mind on something else – maybe something else they too could have weighed up thoroughly before leaving home?

You see, once you start looking at the follow-throughs, the knock-ons, the what ifs, you're on the way to developing Pause Button thinking into a habit. And, as we said before, you just need 21, maybe 30 days' intensive training and you'll be doing it without a second thought!

However long-winded it seems in the writing, we'd suggest it's actually a lot easier (and quicker) to spot the consequences of your choices in practice. But it is most certainly something you need to practise. From now on, or whenever you decide you want to start making changes, take those few seconds at each and every choice point. Each and every decision. Yes, each and every decision. It might seem like mental overkill, or a waste of time, or just plain bonkers. But please do try to consider every choice you have to make really, really carefully. Go into slow-motion to see your options ahead of you. Allow things to glide slowly past, in full detail. Look at the two roads – the 'what if I do' and the 'what if I don't' – never forgetting it's not just about how it affects you, it's about how things might snowball to affect everyone around you.

Back to the car. You arrive at work. Choice of parking spaces? Trivial? How about if you know you're due to leave work late and it'll be scarily dark and deserted in the car park when you need to go to your car? Might you think of parking nearer the building? What if you do take those few moments to consider your options and what difference they might mean to you and your family? Another Pause Button moment. Not one that'll stop you losing your temper with the kids yet? Don't rule out the possibility – because from the moment you start questioning, reasoning, weighing up all your actions and decisions, you'll begin to realize the world of choice available to you.

A PAUSE BUTTON MOMENT

Just for a moment, let's look at something completely different. When you're doing Advanced Driver Training with a police-trained instructor, you are taught a particular technique called Commentary Driving[5] to help you with awareness of all the hazards around you. As you watch a video of a car journey, you're told to narrate out loud, for the whole class to hear, everything you can see ahead of you, as if you were driving the car on screen. It takes quite a lot of concentration even to see the many and various potential hazards – 'Woman with child in buggy on left pavement, bus approaching stop ahead on right, motorbike about to overtake on inside, visible in wing mirror, amber light ahead, three cars at junction, first about to move out in front of me –' and so on.

Authors who've hit writers' block are sometimes encouraged to find the passage that's proving a problem, remember the moment as they'd planned to present it on the page, and then re-write it in highly magnified detail – from the size of the character's shoes and the volume of the noise of gravel being crunched on the drive to the speed of the windscreen wipers on the approaching van, and so on.

The connection? And how is this relevant? Both are examples of taking a look, in minute detail, at what's happening. Although the first is about speed of narration, in some ways it's almost about putting the images into slow motion.

You could use either or both when trying to come to terms with when you need to employ your Pause Button. Pay much – much – more attention to what you do and say, what those around you do and say, and it won't be long before you realize you're generally much more aware. Of everything. Which will allow you to be more mindful.

Which in turn should make pressing Pause, looking at consequences and improving your life in the present, a great deal easier.

You don't *have* to make snap judgements or poor decisions. No one can make those calls, those choices, but you, and if you *choose* to allow yourself Pause Button time, who can stop you? For sure it'll only be you.

And guess what? Something else good will follow. Gaining control is a good feeling. Once you know you can do it, you'll feel more confident in trying again. When you try again and succeed, the upward spiral will continue. Control breeds confidence, breeds success, breeds control, etc. Definitely the right way to be going!

So, you've arrived at work. How many times have you had a verbal run-in with your boss because the first thing you do is make a coffee... but not for her? Maybe today's the day you start thinking through the consequences of that battle. Does it mean she will have you top of the list for a good annual report? At least not bottom of the list? Weigh up your options. Do you make her a coffee without resentment for the first time, knowing that maybe you're prepared to do it occasionally provided some time you get to say your piece about it not being part of your job description – and she'll listen because she knows you've been helpful rather than uncooperative? It's what's sometimes known as swings and roundabouts. Use your Pause Button to think it through: chances are you might still not make that coffee, but at least you've a better insight and realize the possible consequences.

Lunchtime. You go out into the city. Meet a friend. You go for a snack together. He's in a bad mood and starts to tell you all sorts of indiscreet things about a mutual friend. Who should press Pause? Should he? Safeguard the private details of the friend? Safeguard his relationship with them? Prevent the gossip spreading? Or should you be the one to press Pause? Be firm with him, explain it's doing neither of you any good and you'd rather chat about something upbeat to get him in a better mood? Maybe not classic Pause Button, but just stop and think. What's going to give the better outcome? For either/both of you? Remember, it's all about consequences. Taking responsibility for your actions by seeing choices through in the Pause Button safe zone.

As we said earlier, a habit takes a while to create and a while to break. You could look at it (making a new habit on purpose) as creating a path through the jungle. Initially you have to hack your way through, struggle past every clinging weed or branch. The next time you go that way, you'll probably still need to take a tool or a stick with you, to move things out of your way. The following time it'll be relatively straightforward; you'll hardly even need to look where you're putting your feet. After a few more trips down the same route, the path will be wider, maybe even weedless. In time, it'll seem like a highway!

> *'Habits are at first cobwebs, then cables.'*
> **SPANISH PROVERB**

Of course, the reverse will be true if you decide to give up on a habit. Don't use that path and it'll get weedier, narrower and, in time, will once more become completely impassable.

Right now, though, you're trying to create a new, good habit and make it so ingrained it's almost as if it were an instinctive response to be used any time you might need to make a choice.

Research published in summer 2011 by scientists from Duke University in North Carolina suggested that, in fact, the ability to weigh up reward against cost is actually programmed into a specific part of the brain – the dorsal anterior cingulate cortex. The research related to macaque monkeys, who seem to know when to stop grazing from a particular area because the time spent 'working' to get berries from bushes achieves diminishing results. It's been dubbed the 'quit instinct'.[6]

Maybe it's not too great a step to ponder whether that, too, is the part of the brain responsible for weighing up consequences in many other circumstances. Unfortunately, the research only dealt with 'quit now' situations.

'To change a habit requires a combination of acknowledging what you actually do which constitutes your old, "bad" behaviour, bringing it back into the realms of conscious action. That way you can't just conveniently "overlook it". The second part is, of course, to create a new habit – to do something until it becomes second nature.

'PBT can help with both. Pause. Do you realize what you're doing? The consequences? (Fast Forward, Rewind, Pause). You'll be getting preferable outcomes if you continue to do this instead. You know that, don't you?! So do it!'

Let's go back to the day that started with considering whether you've said goodbye nicely.

Your phone rings. It's a very angry customer. Very angry indeed. Off the scale. Question 1: Should *they* learn about PBT to ensure their complaints are heard properly? Question 2: Will your way of dealing with their enquiry be different if you give yourself a moment to consider? Will your supervisor notice you being incredibly calm and pleasant, setting a good example to more junior staff around you? Or will they hear you flustered and unsure how to cope? What will the customer's view of your company be?

There is a natural inclination (even writing this, knowing its significance, you can't help but think) to wonder exactly how relevant any of this really is; how much repetitive 'stop and think' we really expect you to do. The truth is, it's your call. If you want to put a stop to most, maybe all, of your dodgy judgements, you have to give yourself thinking time. Breathing space. A moment or two to consider. And we're proposing PBT is the way to go – and telling you the best way to achieve it.

To some, suggesting that PBT needs to become so habitual as to be virtually instinctive would be repetitive. Others would suggest it's a contradiction in terms. Either way, there are actions that require very little thought; there are behaviours that can be triggered and behaviours that follow flawed psychological triggers.

Taking the bigger picture, we would simply suggest that your questionable choices may be the result of triggers, flawed triggers, or learned behaviour. Or they may be the result of instinct 'subtypes'.

Instinct Subtypes

When working through your PBT process, it might help to recognize that, according to the Enneagram Institute, personality typing[7], instincts themselves can vary depending on events within your development as a child. They all tell of our inbuilt survival requirements. From the three subtypes – self-preservation, social, and sexual – everyone will have stronger influences from one than the others. Genetics is one obvious factor determining the likely personality type of a child, but our personality actually reflects aspects of many factors, influencing development.

1. **Self-preservation** relates to issues of personal survival, encompassing the basics of food, shelter and warmth, plus security and comfort.

2. **Social** is concerned with community, social and group structures and functions, and extends to status and social acceptance.

3. **Sexual**, though not necessarily exclusively referring to relationships involving sexual acts, refers to intensity, closeness and union in vital one-to-one pair bonding.

The benefit of understanding how your behaviours, your emotional priorities, can have been built or influenced by the strengths and weaknesses in different developmental periods in your life, is that you are then better placed to recognize when that historical 'conditioning' starts to kick in in your present-day behaviour.

They may be happening for many different reasons. This (almost!) doesn't matter. What matters today is that you want to change, and that unlearning your habit/addiction/flawed choices, or learning other behaviours in their place by seeing how your life could be better today and tomorrow, will be made so much easier if you press Pause.

So, like it or not, maybe you're realizing that to help you best, PBT needs to become like second nature. So yes, we do think you've got to work, work hard, and start working NOW!!!

Want to stop biting your nails? It might take you three or four weeks. Want to change the rest of your life by cutting out all that over-reaction? It might take you three or four weeks. Examples from the opposite end of the spectrum, but habit-breaking/habit-forming all the same. Simple. OK, in truth it might take you three or four weeks to make a change, but by repeating the PBT method over and over again, you reach a total transformation of your life in a few months. Won't that extra time be worth it?

What's Wrong with Gut Instinct?

Using gut instinct may be more logical than spending a long time evaluating – running through pros and cons, and so on. Not least because if you work against your 'instinctive' responses, you could damage your self-belief. Even affect your ability to make decisions as easily in the future.

We'd argue that if you've got into questionable situations in the past, at least some, and possibly most, of these situations must have, by definition, gone against your 'gut' response, because an understanding of what's 'right', 'best', 'better' and so forth is inherent. Inherent, but not necessarily sufficient to overcome the inertia created by 'here and now' thinking. There isn't enough power to the gut instinct to fight the powerful effects of a desire for instant gratification.

Better then to train yourself by pressing Pause when others might suggest gut instinct would be enough. See into the future with Fast Forward. Decide which of the two or more outcomes are going to be best for you, and only then make your choice. Repeat this process for however long you need to; and, with the process, you're actually not eroding your belief in yourself, you're empowering yourself to know you can make the right choice. *You* can make that choice. No one got in your way. You *can* make that choice. No flawed thinking put you off. How much more likely, then, that you'll go through that process confidently for the foreseeable future, growing in confidence with each change you make until your instinct is almost imperceptibly wound up in pressing Pause, without even realizing it!

> *Impulse control = delayed gratification.*
> *This means you have faced, understood,*
> *and got rid of here-and-now thinking.*

So, Tell Me How to Create This New Habit...

Do you want to know how to create that (good, productive) habit? Start now.

- The very next thing you have to do, have to say, have to react to, crook that finger, press that thumb and give yourself time to look at the consequences if you do *this* and if you do *that.* Think it and feel it – right through to all the possible outcomes.
- Then, and only then, make your decision.
- Repeat.

At some point – maybe days, maybe weeks into the future – you'll realize that, just like learning to drive, you're actually stopping to think, to press your Pause Button, *without* having to 'tell yourself' to do it.

There are many tricks to creating/breaking a habit. The first is to recognize what we have just said. Breaking a habit is effectively just creating a new one.

- Practise often!
- Be realistic about progress – Rome wasn't built in a day.
- Find yourself some triggers. Using your card or thumb to press Pause will help.
- Get family or friends on board to keep you focused.
- It's easier to replace an old habit because the brain is kept busy creating new neural pathways.
- Remember the consequences. Remember the consequences!!!

> *'Motivation is what gets you started.*
> *Habit is what keeps you going.'*
> **JIM RYUN**

As you perform any action on a repeat basis, your reaction time gets faster and faster. The same as the athlete's training regime, or the drills of learning speed typing. Do something often enough and fast enough and you'll acquire the skills to do it really well, almost automatically, and at increasing speeds.

You remember we said you should press Pause at every choice you had to make? That you'd think the idea bonkers? After a while you've probably realized the more you do it, the easier it is to do, and the easier it is to filter out those choices you don't usually have a problem with.

When you use the PBT card, or wristband, or whatever anchor you've opted for, it's performing a function a little like a rosary, or clicking away at worry beads. The repetitive use of it helps you get out of the thinking mind and into the being mind. Hindus and Buddhists often use a set of beads to help them keep count when they're chanting a mantra.

Never forget that, not only are you wanting to wipe away old habits — taking that trip to the casino, overreacting, giving in to alcohol, losing your temper in road rage, threatening your marriage by succumbing to a 'fling', whatever it is — you're also needing to create a replacement habit. That of using PBT. So let's provide yet another explanation of the mechanism for forming a habit.

If you follow the model of Conscious Competence (one of several names),[8] the first stage in any change of behaviour is that of *Unconscious Incompetence*. Here, you literally don't know what you don't know! In other words, you aren't even aware you 'need' or might even want to make a change to your behaviours and actions. There are some who suggest 'unaware' might be a less disparaging term to use than 'incompetent', but we'll stick with the best known.

Conscious Incompetence is the next step. You've identified that you want to do something different. But that's all. You still haven't started the change.

Then comes *Conscious Competence*. You've made changes, but you're still having to keep your eye on the ball to remember to do them.

Finally you reach *Unconscious Competence*. This can be equated to 'automatic pilot', or the sensation of being a long-time driver who goes from point A to point B without really knowing how many times you changed gear, let alone looked in your mirror, performed an overtaking manoeuvre, etc. You just do it without thinking.

Clearly it's that final stage you're aiming at with Pause Button Therapy. And, as you might imagine, there's really only one route to take to get you there. Yes, you must go through those four stages!

It would be very tempting to assume that you, dear reader, have got past Unconscious Incompetence to Conscious Incompetence. In fact, one of the most widely accepted reasons for the failure of teaching/training is that the students don't even realize their own (low) level of skills and the benefits they would get from learning. Without that there can be no progression through the next stages. Most people respond best to training, or only respond to it at all, if they know they need it and what good it will do them.

Do You See Any Need to Change?

Now we are suggesting you stop and think for a while — about what you have read so far and just why you are reading this book. Maybe you are starting to see how, by making just a few changes in your life, you can bring about a number of positive improvements — and possibly not just for you but also for your family and close friends.

So, take a few minutes and rate yourself (truthfully) on the following questionnaire, using a scale of 1–10, with 1 having barely any effect on your life and 10 being something that has a major impact. You should also rate whether or not this affects you rarely, occasionally or often.

	1–10 rating	Frequency	What is the issue?
Have you ever been ashamed of things you have done, involving alcohol, food or drugs?			
Are you ever ashamed of things you have said?			
Have you ever sent a text or email in haste and later regretted it?			
Have you ever phoned or contacted someone while under the influence of alcohol and regretted it later?			
Have you ever been depressed about a repeated behaviour?			
Do you envy other people?			
Has your family ever asked you to change or modify your behaviour in one way or another?			
Has your behaviour ever had a negative effect on your relationship with your partner or with close friends?			
When you think back, can you identify major events/decisions in your life that would have been handled differently if you had invested a little thought?			

When you feel you've answered the questions – and honestly, of course! – sit back and survey the evidence. How much you're being affected by whatever behaviours are at issue should, if not exactly leap from the page, at least be there in black and white. If you didn't think you needed to change, maybe now you're at the point of recognizing that you *do* – and just how much.

What would you give to change that bad habit now? What value would you put on the benefit of changing that habit now?

Is staying in more important than going out? Is continuing to eat fatty foods more important to you than shedding excess weight and feeling healthier? Is living longer more important to you than quitting your nicotine habit? All these last questions are just reminding you of what we said earlier about calculating the value of changing versus the value of not changing. It's a sum only you can do. Now's the time to do it.

Take a long hard look at the blanks in the following two lines. Give yourself a mark for each. Maybe out of 10, maybe out of 50. That's entirely up to you. But it's a sure-fire way to focus your thinking.

- The value I place on ....
  (e.g. continuing to smoke) is ....
- The value I place on ....
  (e.g. having an extra seven healthy years of life) is ....
  ....

To be honest, only you can fill in these blanks, which will help you figure out the values you place on change. We hope this book has helped start that process!

Basically, you need to reflect for a bit on where you are right now in your life and what, if anything, you want to achieve from learning to press Pause. Maybe now, after that reflection (itself a variation on the use of the Pause Button!), you can say you're *Consciously Incompetent* and in fact on the verge of being able to move on. You know you want to make changes – you just haven't done anything about it yet.

Conscious Competence is the one you need to tackle now. It will mean taking as long as you need going through the PBT process. Using thumb and forefinger, or a PBT device, or a home-made card, or a redundant real remote control, you need to put the theory into practice and press Pause whenever and wherever you need to make a decision that has previously foxed you.

Finally, you complete the basic cycle by achieving *Unconscious Competence* – something akin to being on autopilot. You can steer yourself through all those crisis points and triggers, and approaching disastrous choices, putting PBT into FFW, Play and REW without even thinking about it.

And how did you manage all that? By repeating the process over and over again. You know the score by now. It's just a question of doing it often enough that it becomes an unconscious action or series of actions.

There's a user-friendly way of describing this process of change:

- You don't know what you don't know.
- You know what you don't know.
- You're trying to learn it.
- It's second nature.

Of course, in attempting to enact these changes in your life, moving through the 'Conscious Competence' model, you may well find you slip back from one step to the previous one – maybe even slip back two steps if you lose focus for a while. Then it's just a case of re-addressing the move 'up' from one stage to the next, re-learning your motivation, and so on, as you go.

Never forget: failure can simply be another step on the road to success.

Having established without question that you know you want to make a change – you do, don't you?! – let's take a look at how to create that more constructive habit than whatever's causing you headaches and heartache at the moment.

Recognize that there's a crisis point coming, or a decision to be made, or anger rising; or that there's an overwhelming temptation to make a hasty comment, send a critical text, a sarcastic email. Recognize the need to stop, and press Pause. Literally, with thumb and forefinger.

Just do it. Take a deep breath if it'll help. But press that Pause Button!

Now you're safely in your chosen haven, your zone away from outside influences, and time has stopped still. Nothing and no one can get to you. This place is somewhere of your making, your choice. You might carry a visual image of where you are – a much-loved garden, or a windswept beach – or you might just have a mental 'rest area', a bit like a cocoon where you literally have breathing space. You're free to think what you want and consider what you want. And what you need to do, if you're honest. What you should spend this 'safe time' doing is looking at the consequences of what you were about to do.

So press Fast Forward – Pause. Look at what's happening. Feel what you're feeling. See how things seem. Then Rewind, Pause, Fast Forward and Pause again to experience the consequences if you take a different course of action. How does that feel? How are your loved ones feeling? Give yourself enough time to fully take in the sensation at that point. You can then Rewind, Pause and make your decision to Play things out – i.e. get on with your morning, your day, your life! – having a clear view of the consequences of your choice.

Next time, make sure you remember – trigger yourself – to do it again. Yes, of course that was repeating ourselves. We're good at that!

> *'That which we persist in doing becomes easier –*
> *not that the nature of the task has changed,*
> *but our ability to do it has increased.'*
> **RALPH WALDO EMERSON**

In case you're in any doubt about the process of learning and unlearning habits, bear in mind that researchers have actually done experiments on brain activity during the process of learning. Subjects were placed in MRI scanners and given a sequence of keystrokes on a normal keyboard to learn. Then their brain activity was monitored.[9]

In the initial steps, having to remember the sequence to start with, the whole brain is 'alight' with the effort. The forebrain contains various high-level planning and memory areas, including the prefrontal cortex and premotor cortex. All seemed to be involved. In fact, large areas of the brain were involved in learning the sequence – even the cerebellum, previously believed to be only concerned with motor reflex.

Once the sequence was 'memorized', though, the brain activity seemed to peter out. Oxygenated blood, being tracked by the scanner, was no longer being targeted by as many parts of the brain – suggesting fewer areas were 'busy'. Only a small number of 'motor' areas of the brain remained involved in moving the fingers. The researchers condensed their findings to the perception that having used the whole brain to establish the individual finger movements required, the routine was then 'converted' to form what was described as a skeletal crust of habit. A fixed and autonomous memory.

The subjects' brains seemed to have developed a template to short-circuit having to go through all the more complex details of remembering the sequence each and every time.

Maybe, then, we have none of those excuses we trot out for not giving up cigarettes, or altering our diet to shift a few excess pounds. Our brains will cope admirably with the change of behaviour pattern – given just a bit of time. Say, 21 days?

A PAUSE BUTTON MOMENT

Panic attacks stop Allan from living his life. He describes feeling his heart racing, being unable to breathe, feeling dizzy and sweaty and generally out of control. At times he thinks he is going to die. He has started avoiding places or situations that he thinks will trigger his anxiety. His therapist introduced him to PBT, and now, using the technique, he can stop his mind from running on. He can freeze time, take a breath and understand what is happening within his mind. He can visualize the end of a panic attack, when everything has calmed down. He doesn't need to see two alternative scenarios – just seeing one shows him everything is actually going to be fine. All he needs to do is stop, relax, breathe slowly and everything will eventually come back under his control again.

IN THIS CHAPTER YOU'VE LEARNED:

- Have you recognized your old, negative behaviour? Identified the behaviour you'd prefer to use?
- Start clearing that path through the jungle. Soon it'll become easier and easier.
- Visualizing consequences.

*Pause * Think * Decide * Act*

PART 3
PBT IN PRACTICE

HOW DO *YOU* USE
THE REMOTE?

*'The secret of achievement is to hold a picture of a
successful outcome in the mind.'*
HENRY DAVID THOREAU

A remote control device is something the general public has
used to avoid 'unnecessary' physical exertions for over 50
years – since its development for military use late in the 1940s.
Most widely used for household electronic gadgetry – TVs, DVD
players and so on – the first versions were actually dubbed the
'Lazy Bones' because they ensured no one had to actually stand
up and move to change channels![1]

However, they are now so widely used there can't be many
homes – globally – without at least one remote control device.
Indeed, one manufacturer's survey showed between a third and
half of households have not one but four remotes[2] in the living room.

All of which leads back to how to use the thing! We all have
our way; if you search the web you'll find a multiplicity of images
of index fingers, middle fingers, thumbs and many combinations
used to press the various buttons.

Most, though, seem to indicate that supporting the device diagonally across the palm of your hand and bending your thumb over to do the 'button-pressing' is the most common configuration.

Not for the first time, and chances are, not for the last, you might be thinking, 'Why are we talking about this?' Well, there's a very good reason. Before we go any further, just imagine you've a remote in your hands and you're trying to 'switch off' the person on the other side of the room. Implausible? Humour us. The son/daughter/husband/mother-in-law is filling your head with noise? Thought so. We'd bet good money that it wouldn't take too much imagination to use your hand/thumb, just the way you do in the living room at home! Go on – do it another time. Press Pause!

So why do we want you to do this – again and again – in much the same way as the previous chapter went on about creating habits? Well, in hypnotherapy (and a number of other therapies), professionals like to use what's called an 'anchor' – a tangible means, involving as many senses as possible, to remind and reinforce the 'message' of the therapy in the patient's mind.

You may have heard of would-be non-smokers rubbing their temple whenever they get a cigarette craving? That action is an anchor. Repetition is used to imprint (associate) the rubbing with the change to a particular mental state – relaxed, decisive or fearless, for example. Once that is achieved, you can begin to feel that in your head, in your imagination; you have moved away from the present moment and arrived at a place safe from threat of interruption, intrusion or harm. It can be any kind of place, real or imagined, but it must be as vivid as possible in your mind.

An anchor can in fact be any stimulus that triggers a consistent psychological state; some actually use the term 'trigger' instead of 'anchor', for logical reasons. Particularly appropriate to Pause Button Therapy is the definition some people use that an anchor provides a 'safe place'. In the case of PBT, this is a state of mind in which you cannot be interrupted or distracted, allowing you the opportunity to think things through.

Anchoring was first identified by Pavlov, who rang a bell when about to feed his dog. After much repetition, the dog assumed food was coming and started to salivate when a bell sounded, even if he saw no food. It is now accepted that anchoring, discovered in that most basic of ways, is likely to be a key to success if used in hypnotic techniques.

It usually creates associations between emotions and a trigger, which means situations can be controlled because the mind can be calmed (or brought to whatever state the trigger specifies).

Within the realms of self-hypnosis, rather than stage-show or clinical hypnosis, this offers the opportunity for ordinary, everyday people such as yourself to give themselves unexpected confidence and power.

By identifying something that happened to you and made you feel really good – really confident, successful and unassailable – you can then connect that sensation and those feelings with a pre-determined trigger. From then on it will only need the trigger to bring these empowering feelings up again.

And how is this going to help you? Well, done by yourself or by a therapist, the calming effect of deep relaxation is the basis of all hypnotherapy. There is also obvious potential if you begin to feel anxious, angry or unhappy. Without needing to involve the deep relaxation state, you can use your trigger –

in the case of PBT it need only be a crooked forefinger and pressed thumb – to raise your confidence levels and boost your self-esteem. More than that, though, you can use Pause and Fast Forward to consider the consequences of any action you may choose to take.

Therapists will use whatever sense is likely to provide the strongest response in the client. TV illusionist Derren Brown demonstrated the significance of anchors and triggers when, in a 2006 show (transmitted again in the UK in 2011)[3], he achieved a three-out-of-four success rate in attempting to 'persuade' apparently normal members of the public to stage an 'armed' robbery in central London. The anchors included music, colour and a key phrase, all of which had been 'imprinted' over a series of sessions.

Of course, we hope no one's thinking of armed robbery – we're certainly not! We know Derren Brown wasn't, either. The example of that show, does, though, demonstrate just how key these anchors can be in reinforcing a plan: habit, sound, visual stimuli, repetition, you get the idea!

With PBT, the trigger is pretty much inbuilt in the name of the therapy: it's the visual manifestation (and to some extent tactile, involving the hand/fingers) of the idea that pressing Pause gives you a 'freeze frame' moment. Just like you get in your living room with your TV or DVD, but a 'freeze frame' in your life. Pausing your actions and giving you thinking time.

The point? Well, putting it simply, we developed PBT to echo not only the various elements available within a remote control device, but also to enable you to recognize the sensations of stopping time, moving into Fast Forward, Rewinding and so forth. To achieve this in its entirety it may well be best for you if you can always have your Pause Button to hand to help. But, life being what it is, that probably won't happen each and every time you need to stop and think.

For those moments, and for those people for whom, for whatever reason, a card doesn't really resonate in their head the way it needs to, there's always using your crooked thumb and forefinger as if you were holding a real remote! You could also order a wristband and PBT plastic remote, but you won't have a remote control device in your hand 24/7, so there will be times when you just have to imagine one.

Just think about what happens when you really use a remote control device. You curl your last three fingers to hold it, but the two that matter (and if you do it now, just in your mind, or with your hand, you'll see what we mean) are your crooked index finger and your thumb pointed at that index finger, ready to Press Pause, or Fast Forward, or whatever. Think about it... Now do it... See what we mean? You don't even need the remote to recognize what that very specific hand shape means to every single person who's ever wielded a remote control!

And crooking your forefinger and 'pressing' with your thumb is such a common action that it should be easy to do *without* a remote or other actual prop and still achieve the same (mental) effect. It's just a matter of wishing it to be. And practise!

So – what are you waiting for? Try it! We know of someone who physically went to 'turn down' her chattering son in the back of the car. Actually reached her arm out to adjust the volume control button, simply because the action of using the audio control is such an established part of her driving 'life'.

Not much of a step really to needing a halt in proceedings; to putting a stop to whatever madness is just around the corner, and figuring out that one way to do that is to 'press Pause' – literally!

Again, we'd say 'try it'. Do it in the staff canteen, to see if you can recognize it's possible to stop your thoughts wandering to how much you despise your boss. Do it in the kitchen, when you know you're festering towards a shouting match with your youngsters in the run-up to the evening meal.

Is that shouting going to bring you closer to your children, or distance you? Will you have a tight bond long term if you keep going this way? Is contemplating your boss' shortcomings likely to improve your work performance?

If you can just press Pause. Get used to doing it – pressing your thumb to your crooked forefinger. You know what it feels like. You use it to switch channels umpteen times a day. You use it to turn the volume up; to turn the TV off; to move to an audio track you prefer. You can't pretend (to yourself – no one's fooling us!) that you don't know exactly what we're talking about.

Pause. Easy. Fast forward. Easy. Rewind. Easy.

Crook that finger, press that thumb.

OK, we've got that sorted. Or have we?

When you have developed a behaviour pattern or habit you want to change, there is a high probability that the behaviour itself starts 'on cue' – following triggers itself. For example, you are expecting a call from a business associate. You hear the phone. As you pick it up, you reach for your cigarettes and lighter at exactly the same time. Even the knowledge that a call was expected was cue enough for you to be 'ready and waiting' to smoke that cigarette.

You're home alone, as usual, with your kids. They've played up no more, no less than usual, but enough to trigger in you that desire for a glass (and too many more) of wine once they're safely in bed. You may not actually pour the first glass of wine until you've tucked them up for the night, but the cue was there in your mood, those familiar feelings, in the run-up to bedtime.

Two examples: and you will be able to come up with lots more; not only for yourself, but possibly for people you know. Crucially, though, once you're using Pause Button Therapy, all those cues and triggers can be seen as 'Pause Points'. You're home alone and the kids are playing up and... 'press Pause'. Think through and visualize how you'll feel if you do, and if you don't, have the wine. Once they're in bed, 'press Pause' again. Think through again. As time goes on, even if you eventually give in to your trigger the first few times, you will have taught yourself a major lesson. You *can* think about it. You *can* delay that desire. And sooner or later, you *will* at some stage *not* have that wine.

Ditto the anticipated phone call/cigarette trigger. As soon as you know the call will be coming, press Pause. Visualize whether you'll actually feel less stressed as a result of the smoke, the nicotine, the chemicals, or whether it's a mistaken belief. Visualize whether you'll regret delaying your 'quit day' yet again. Visualize how much more positive you'll be about yourself if you can reduce your daily habit, even by one or two cigarettes. Then later, the phone goes. Press Pause. Now's your chance to visualize big-time how much better you'll feel if you can simply not light up this time. How much of a letdown it would be to 'give in'.

The same kind of story in so many different scenarios.

Because simply wielding that imaginary remote, using your thumb to actually physically press that Pause Button, has given you control over time. Given you the thinking space you didn't believe you had. Put you in a safe zone.

Some people will, as we've said, prefer to hold the actual credit card-sized Pause Button device. Some will prefer to wear their tactile PBT wristband. Others will be absolutely fine simply crooking their forefinger and pressing the 'virtual' remote buttons with their thumb. These are not the only options you could employ, though.

So many homes have surplus, redundant remotes lying around. Why not find one of those and carry it around with you for a week or so, just to have the physical reminder of the possibilities of Pause – Fast Forward – Rewind?

*'If your teeth are clenched and your fists are clenched,
your lifespan is probably clenched.'*
TERRI GUILLEMETS

Or maybe your problem – or a family member's – is impulse shopping? It wouldn't be too difficult to slip your credit or debit card into a small envelope and then put a copy of the Pause Button illustration on the outside. To be able to make that snap purchase you'd *have* to face the Pause Button, and that might be enough to make you stop and consider the consequences of spending that money. You want that half-price designer shirt?

OK, you have to get out your credit or debit card. But before that, you're reminded both visually and physically that maybe you should take a moment to stop and think.

So, hold that envelope and, instead of spending money, press Pause. Think ahead; visualize how you'll feel in a day, week, month if you make the purchase and either the shirt doesn't fit (refunds not allowed during sale period), you decide you don't like it as much as you thought (ditto) or you have a common sense moment and realize your pay cheque was a bit smaller this month because you worked fewer hours, on top of which your car payment is due. Rewind, Fast Forward to what will happen if you *don't* buy it: this time you're less stressed about that car payment, happier that your smaller bank balance will stretch further, pleased you didn't add yet another white shirt to your already overfull wardrobe and – arguably most importantly – you feel more positive because you held out against the impulse.

PBT is not only key to changing individuals' lives. The knock-on effect on family and friends will become apparent soon enough. As you are in the process of learning how to control your decision-making, and how to make more appropriate choices generally, we believe there's all sorts of scope for involving friends and family. Pause Button Therapy has potential applications throughout society, across all age groups, and how much more understanding of the notion of cause and effect, action and reaction, of consequences as a whole, would absolutely everyone in a family be if they all 'joined in'?

If you're familiar with the phrase 'whatever it takes', you should understand our viewpoint when we say it doesn't matter *how* you choose to press Pause. Getting yourself into the imprinted, ingrained, as-near-as-can-be unconscious use of the PBT system – zapping with that remote to Pause yourself – is what counts.

For you, that may mean using one of our suggested methods. You might feel you need an actual remote (maybe even a real, redundant one!). Or you might be someone for whom some kind of oral memory-jogger is the way to go. You feel a choice might be about to be sprung upon you, so you start repeating a sequence of words that tells you to Pause. It might be something as simple as, 'Press Pause, I must Press Pause now. I must Press Pause now and consider the consequences.' You might like to say this *as* you press Pause with your thumb/forefinger, or *as* you press the buttons on your real, plastic or cardboard PBT remote. You might wish to say, 'No one else can stop me but me. Press Pause now, [your name].' Just think of the brilliant feeling that control will bring you.

The method chosen really doesn't need to have any relevance or effectiveness for anyone apart from you. If you can really get 'into' this, you may well find you can customize quite specifically. Your word sequence might be better for you if whispered under your breath, or you might need to do something approaching a mantra. You may feel happier not letting a sound cross your lips. You may have a tune you associate with peace, tranquillity and calm contemplation. If you let that come to mind when you are pressing Pause, it might help. It's entirely personal.

Use the remote, in whatever form *you've* chosen, the way that best suits *you*.

A PAUSE BUTTON MOMENT

Mike and Sally have been drifting apart. When they first got married there was a regular routine when Mike came home from work: they would have their dinner together and sit and talk about the day, before sitting down to enjoy a film or TV programme together. The weekends would be spent shopping, doing DIY or visiting family or friends. The relationship started to break down after Sally was introduced to a group of old friends via social networking sites. Not only was she 'talking' to old friends – and boyfriends, which didn't go down very well with Mike – but she became wrapped up in her online life and increasingly withdrew from her day-to-day relationships, going online after dinner and going to bed long after Mike.

When Mike heard about PBT from someone at work, and suggested they both start working with PBT, Sally learned to press Pause and see the consequences of her 'virtual' life. By Fast Forwarding to how she and Mike could once again be closer, and enjoy the things they used to do together, she was able to think of planning for the future without resorting to living an online life.

IN THIS CHAPTER YOU'VE LEARNED:

- Crook that finger, press that thumb.

- Get the kids involved!

- Visualizing consequences.

Pause * Think * Decide * Act

CHANGING YOUR MIND

*'If you change the way you look at things,
the things you look at change.'*
DR WAYNE DYER

By now you should be clear in your mind that you're experiencing consequences you don't like. You've realized that your actions and reactions have a part to play. Although other people may be contributing, you have to look to your own behaviour, change your own patterns.

Do you accept that you've got to the point of wanting to change? Do you know the ways in which you want to change? Your next step must be to accept that, if you're going to actually start to change rather than just thinking about it, you must attempt to pinpoint whatever it is that kick-starts your own personal cause-effect cycle. You need to try to understand your thought processes.

Everything but everything you do begins with a thought. Everything. Not much thought goes into it, sometimes! But there's a nanosecond's thought there all the same. Adjusting the waistband of your trousers. Dashing off to get a coffee. Stroking the cat. Deciding which word follows the last while

writing. All those actions, and millions of others, start with a thought. Quite clearly, some of those thoughts could be put down to conditioned responses, or habitual actions – things we've talked about already. However you label these, though, what it boils down to is that some part of you has had to – albeit fleetingly – be aware of and compute what you're about to do.

You could define that thought as a response to a stimulus, a pattern following rules. You could discuss the part played by neurons, and whether or not their role is the more important aspect of any thought process. Or you could say to yourself, 'All I need to know, really, is that I think, therefore I am', demonstrating you can quote Descartes, but not proving much else! Or possibly none of these thoughts would enter your head, and even if they did, they'd just confuse you? Essentially, what you need to come to terms with is that you've put a bit of thought in, maybe a little, maybe a lot, maybe barely any at all (and that's the problem), before every single action you've taken.

From hypothesis to Gestalt psychology, and from instinct to interpretation, analogy, argument and attitude, mind mapping, morphological analysis and multi-tasking – there is a veritable alphabet[1] of styles, methods and types of thought.

In truth, you don't need to know much about how your thoughts might be defined or labelled by academics. If you can understand how *your* thoughts work, what processes are involved in *your* head – no one else's matter, after all – you stand a better chance of slipping a Pause Button moment in where it would be helpful.

In his book *Stop Thinking, Start Living,*[2] Richard Carlson works a strong core theme – thoughts are just that. They are not facts;

they are your own product. You manufacture them, and any power should be in the direction of you exerting power over your thoughts, not the other way round. Thoughts have no power to influence or rule your life.

In a similar way to how CBT says you need to recognize illogical or negative automatic thinking, as opposed to rational response, Carlson suggests the following. When something happens you wish hadn't, if you think, 'How awful, things never go right for me', you actually start a vicious cycle of self-pity, more negative thinking, and so on. To get away from this you need to recognize that it was only a thought. 'How awful, things never go right for me' is clearly nothing more than a thought. It can't possibly be anything else. It's not a fact. It's just a thought you have manufactured in response to something that has occurred. The only fact is that something occurred – that event you wish hadn't. The thought itself isn't a fact. It cannot harm you. Get to grips with that and you will give yourself the chance to recognize negative thoughts when they happen in the future. And recognizing them means you can dismiss them in the way they deserve!

> *'In the beginning there was a thought.'*
> **DESCARTES**

Triggers

We've mentioned that substance abuse – and indeed, most if not all addictive behaviours – involves some element of a trigger. A pattern – a predictable though possibly unrecognized action which leads to the use of the substance.

To help identify what your particular triggers are, we'd suggest you try a memory-jogger used by newspaper reporters to ensure they've covered every aspect of a story:

Who – What – When – Where – Why – How

Think about when you last took a drink, or injected, or binged, or purged, or checked the light switches 17 times before leaving home, and then ask yourself this sequence of questions.

- **Who** was I with? Is it always the same person? Or the same type of person?
- **What** was I doing just before the 'need' kicked in?
- **When** did it happen? Was it the same day, or the same time of day as normal?
- **Where** was I? Should I try to avoid that place?
- **Why** do I feel, deep down, that I chose to drink/inject/etc.?
- **How** did I get the drink/drugs/etc.?

  and also

- **How** did I feel half an hour later? An hour later? The following morning?

With your answers to these questions, if you address them each time you use, you'll be creating a picture of your addiction; very likely a pattern will emerge, giving you the means to make it less likely you'll put yourself in that situation again.

There are usually people, places and things that can be identified as 'constants'. For example, you always spend time with the same people, go to the same places, do the same things, and this often leads to an addict using or lapsing.

Always seem to be with the chap from accounts when you end up having an after-work drinking session? Avoid him! Develop other friendships! Always get the drink or drugs when you're driving around at the weekend? Cut out the particular outing that leads you past your usual 'dealer' zone. When do you mostly use/abuse? In the evenings, after you've tidied everything away and have free time to sit about aimlessly? Change your housework timetable! Take up a hobby!

Do these suggestions sound trite? Of course they do. Be honest: you're thinking this doesn't apply to you, or that changing your weekend drive won't make a scrap of difference, or even, 'Me? Addicted?'

Well, not a bit of it. Be honest a bit longer. You're almost guaranteed to see patterns showing up if you admit to the full picture. Did you read that? If you've been honest, you should see patterns emerging. Indeed, you didn't really need to be asked – you know already.

Once you recognize your particular patterns, you can re-draw them to make it less likely you'll fall prey to your addictive moments. And once you know your 'triggers', you can press Pause when you know they're about to be set off. Spend time looking at the consequences, good and bad, and then make an informed choice rather than a knee-jerk reaction simply because it's Friday, you're with Joe and a line of cocaine awaits.

We firmly believe there probably isn't a behavioural problem, issue or addiction that can't be successfully treated using PBT. We've picked a few of the more obvious ones to illustrate how your thoughts might wind you up to the point where you demonstrate that behaviour, succumb to that addiction. If you recognize any of what follows, this is the first step to changing how you live in the present to the way you would like it – and your future, of course – to be!

Road Rage

If you begin to research road rage – particularly on the Internet – you could easily give up on the human race altogether. There we find a range of people, from those sufficiently in touch with their feelings to recognize the start of that 'red mist' of anger coming over them, to those stating to anyone who'll listen that they believe they have an absolute entitlement to have a gun in their vehicle to get their own back on slow drivers/poor 'junction mergers'/whoever they deem inconsiderate.

One way or another, the mere fact of being shut inside (sometimes over) a tonne of metal makes some people feel invincible, and wholly entitled to the belief that they should have a clear road to the exclusion of all others. It's described as a 'trance-like state' for some; akin to a hypnotic state triggered simply by sitting behind the wheel of your vehicle. But this anger response is a conditioned response, every bit as much as Pavlov's dog was.

Experiences in life can sometimes unintentionally cause conditioned responses. If you happen to get a stomach upset when out fishing with your brother, any future smell of fish might provoke sickness. That coincidence of a negative experience – the stomach upset – leads to the creation of an association that causes the learned behaviour (sickness at the smell of fish). New conditioning – maybe linking the scent of fish with positive experiences – can overcome the earlier response.

To progress with the changes you're looking to make in your life, PBT can help if you press Pause and recognize where (in the case of road rage) your bad, vengeful, angry feelings will get you. Do you really want someone you possibly know in the car next to you to see your face contorted in anger? Do you really want your sweet innocent child in the back booster seat to learn words she didn't know before?

Or – Rewind and Fast Forward again – would you rather she learned the benefits of patience, of understanding you can't make the traffic change just for you. Or recognizing the dangers of lane-hopping; the effect on your blood pressure of honking your horn at everyone who has the cheek to pull in front of you?

Drug Abuse

Many experts in the field have many different views on this subject, and some believe a long-term drug user/abuser will have experienced a change in their brain chemistry, effectively making them unable to take control of their actions without outside intervention.

Not all addicts are in denial that they have a problem, and those who acknowledge the problem are demonstrating a real awareness that can be worked with. This acknowledgement/awareness also implies an understanding of 'normal', and 'acceptable' behaviours – without that understanding, the drug abuse would be unlikely to be seen as a problem.

While acknowledging that a drug user might be a 'hard core' client, Martin is certain there is still scope for PBT to step in and play a part. He believes every addiction involves planning, and at the moment someone has the first, tiniest thought about how they are going to get their hit for the evening, or where they put their dealer's number in their mobile, or whether or not their parent/partner will be at home later when they want to score a hit – all these moments are potential Pause moments. If just one user, every so often, starts to delay or put off a single use of that drug of choice, he says this should be viewed as a definite success.

As Gay Jones feels, all habits have a benefit: some good, some bad. In the case of drugs, the user would be working with PBT to change that benefit from 'good', as they see it, to 'bad' when viewed through the PBT lens, while on Pause, assessing all the consequences on their health, bank balance, job, home life, family and so on. They need to switch to acknowledging that the consequences they actually prefer would be those that come from *not* taking the drug. Effectively, to change from a habit with not one but many bad pay-offs to one (the habit of pressing Pause and giving themselves thinking time) with very obvious good pay-offs.

Easier said than done? Acknowledged. But remember Martin's point – every single drug not taken, even if it only reduces the intake by a small percentage, is to the good. And every time the user presses their Pause Button it will be boosting their self-belief and increasing their confidence that yes, one day, they can regain full control of their life. Every step of control achieved then boosts the virtuous circle.

Alcohol

There's not a huge difference between the alcohol-dependent person and the drug addict. Sounds implausible? Maybe, but, looking away from the chemical influences, the alcohol-dependent person may not even be aware of the psychological triggers that can bring about the feeling of a need to drink. Going through the PBT process – learning to press Pause, viewing the consequences, recognizing that their own triggers exist – can only help the process of self-knowledge; of understanding their habit and how to change it.

'Our troubles, we think, are basically of our own making. They arise out of ourselves, and the alcoholic is an extreme example of self-will run riot, though he usually doesn't think so.[3]'
ALCOHOLICS ANONYMOUS

In the same way as with giving up cigarettes or drugs, the alcohol-dependent person might not immediately give up completely. But with every Pause Button moment that leads to one less drink, the improvement will become apparent and, moreover, that ability to regain control, as mentioned earlier, will boost self-esteem.

Anger Management

At times, 40-year-old Geoff felt he really struggled with reactional anger. He used his mobile phone for everything – calls, texts, emails and the Internet. After a very long and difficult day at his office, he received a blunt, badly worded text from a very close colleague. After the day he'd had, his reaction was very angry and, instead of calming himself down before he responded to the text, he sent a similarly toned text back.

The consequences were massive: an interview with his line manager and a postponement of his expected promotion. Having recognized he had an issue with anger, Geoff looked for guidance from PBT. Every time he could sense he was about to lose his cool, he learned to press Pause and consider his next actions. He would then use those few 'frozen' moments to look a few minutes into the future to see how his typical reaction would result in bad consequences. He started to use the concept of the 'fork in the road' to see that there are (at least) two options for how to react. He now takes 'time out' before he responds.

Of course, Geoff's example is by no means an isolated one. Imagine yourself, or someone you know, standing at a bar, having a beer with a friend. Someone comes in between you, knocking over your beer, which goes everywhere. You could turn round and tell the guy he's an idiot. There's a chance then you'd get a smack on the chin. You could stamp on his foot – react however you want before the guy's even had a chance to apologize or explain what happened or why it happened.

Or, of course, you could start thinking about doing it in a different way. One that won't involve a fight, won't mean you not being able to go back to that bar again, won't affect how your wife thinks about you going for a drink with that particular friend again because she thinks wherever he goes he attracts trouble. Now *that* would be the Pause Button way!

Self-harm

Lucy, a 19-year-old, was self-harming. She had lost all hope and was desperate for something to change. She already knew there were many emotional issues going on in her mind, and that the self-harming was only part of it. Like many who self-harm, she found her actions gave her a mixture of escape, relief and control. Also, like most, she kept her suffering to herself and practised self-harm in private. It was a kind of self-soothing mechanism for her.

Yet every time she ended up self-harming, Lucy felt a lot worse – a pattern seen in several problem behaviours. The guilt and worry she was left with afterwards were only adding to the shame she felt, which was then followed by another act of harm to deal with those feelings. Lucy was on a downward spiral and didn't know what to do to stop it.

With PBT, Lucy was encouraged to press Pause whenever she felt the urge to self-harm. That act of 'freezing time' put her in a safe place; somewhere she didn't feel she *had* to act because nothing could 'get at' her. She could then

Fast Forward to recognize the negative thoughts she would be feeling within five minutes of her actions. She'd see the consequences in the form of possibly permanent marks on her body. A visual reminder of a bad time in her life. She'd see boyfriends, relatives, trying to avoid looking at the marks to spare her feelings.

She also had the 'safe space' while on Freeze Frame to consider alternative, less harmful actions, such as squeezing ice cubes, eating a chilli or having a cold shower. In truth, she could even spend time 'frozen' knowing that if, in five minutes, she still wanted to self-harm, those few moments needn't stop her.

However, the choice was hers. Those moments thinking were hers. No one else could change anything or do anything; it was time for her to think things through, and thoroughly see and feel the consequences of any action she decided to take. That space – that magnifying glass to see where her actions might lead her and how they'd make her feel – was very empowering. Being able to then Rewind back to the present and realize that, this time, she hadn't immediately acted on her impulse and had thought through future feelings, began to build her confidence and sense of responsibility.

She acknowledged that to manage not to hurt herself would be a really hopeful and powerful step. And that, even if she hadn't succeeded, at least she knew she had the tools to intercept her thought process. She had taken 'time out', and maybe next time would be successful and she wouldn't self-harm.

The more Lucy practised using PBT, the easier it got.

Although she is succeeding in self-harming less often, Lucy is also exploring in therapy her pain, and the emotions that make her feel the need to act in this way. She is learning to develop better ways of calming herself down, and is now focusing on more positive things and learning to express her anger, sadness and fear in healthier ways. She is starting to feel more in control of her life.

Self-harm can take several forms[4]. Someone may:

- take too many tablets – an overdose
- cut themselves
- burn their body
- bang their head or throw their body against something hard
- punch themselves
- stick things in their body
- swallow inappropriate objects.

Self-harmers often do so to show someone their distress or to reduce feelings of tension and relieve guilt; it is seen as a 'quick fix' when they feel bad. Very occasionally, it can even be used to get back at someone else, or punish them.

It would be too easy to assume that self-harm is a cool, deliberate action, complete with regular planning in the way someone who's alcohol dependent 'plans' by having spare drink in the house, or time alone to drink to excess without anyone knowing. However, self-harm is more often done when the self-harmer is emotional or distressed. Even though some may plan, it can also happen suddenly.

Obsessive Compulsive Disorder

There is a wide spectrum of OCD symptoms.[5] These include obsessions (thoughts or feelings that bring distress or anxiety) and compulsions (actions that make the sufferer feel they can cancel the obsession). You can have either or both, or more than one type of either or both.

Common obsessions are: believing that objects are dirty/contaminated; worry about health/hygiene; fear about safety/security (unlocked doors/windows, appliances left on); preoccupation with order/symmetry; hoarding; thoughts of aggression/sex; and religion/anti-religion.

The compulsive behaviours, which sufferers use to offset the anxiety of the obsessions, may be physical or mental and usually have some connection to the obsessional element. For example: checking locks, taps, gas; washing hands; repeated specific acts; repeating phrases in the head; ordering the symmetry of objects around you; and hoarding useless items. Sufferers often believe some terrible outcome will befall them if they don't fulfil their compulsion. Carrying out the compulsion gives short-term good feelings, which don't last.

Sufferers usually know that their thoughts/actions – which can be time-consuming and get in the way of normal work and home life – are unreasonable, and often feeling guilty or embarrassed.

Liz, 35, had begun to find that her daily routine and obsessions were destroying her day-to-day living and relationships. Even going out to work or for a walk were becoming too difficult because, in her compulsion/obsession, everything had to be done 10 times and in a certain way. Counting to 10 was something Liz did with everything; she even chewed her food 10 times before she swallowed it. Leaving the house was now proving too hard to do and this was stopping her from living her life. These obsessions and rituals didn't feel like a choice for Liz; they felt like they were the only way to cope.

With PBT she learned to press Pause for a few seconds, just before she carried out her 'counting to 10' rituals. She put herself on Freeze Frame and gave herself the safe space to consider different options and to really understand the consequences of the actions she was continually taking.

She began to realize her actions hadn't actually been affecting how she felt at all. In fact, they were making her feel worse – more like a failure. She felt strangely remorseful that, even though she'd succeeded in not counting, life was still there for her to get on with.

Liz learned that she had choices, if only she stopped to consider them. Every time she had the need/urge to act in her ritual routines, she would press Pause. This didn't always work – sometimes she continued acting on her compulsion – but it became clear to her that it was helping her to postpone her actions and giving her time to think.

Pausing and thinking soon became another way of living for Liz, and within a few months her obsessive-compulsive behaviour started to reduce.

Now Liz is working through her issues in a very supportive therapeutic relationship with her counsellor, and she feels she has more control and choices in her life.

Panic Attacks

Everyone will of course be different, but in general the thought process of anyone prone to panic attacks will start with an incident that leads the sufferer to start a process of questioning.[6] What is questioned will depend on the individual. It might be that they have a plane journey to take. They *know* a crash is statistically unlikely, but nonetheless allow doubt to creep in. Or a situation is coming up and they want to know what's going to happen.

How will it impact on them? Will they be able to deal with whatever is ahead? Uncertainty arising from not being able to find answers (or, conceivably, doubting the answers provided) rapidly compounds the feelings of helplessness. Once the questioning and uncertainty have started to create fear, the vicious circle is well on its course. It is only a matter of time before they start to panic.

So how can PBT help? Clearly the time to press Pause is *before* fear turns to panic – and obviously the earlier the better. So, if you recognize the feelings of mounting breathlessness, throbbing in the ears or palpitations in the early phases, before they even get to the panic stage, so much the better.

We feel that you would benefit at any point throughout an attack from pressing Pause and thinking about what you are doing. Ask yourself, 'Am I really about to have a heart attack? Am I going to die right here? Is it true I can't breathe or am I just making a fool of myself and everybody's looking at me?' Ask the question, 'Has anyone ever died from a panic attack?'

Better to test the theory, 'Where is the empirical evidence for what I'm thinking? How will I feel in 10 minutes when I've calmed down and have to talk to my companions about what brought this on? Will I feel totally unable to control my emotions *again*? No, I know I'll be feeling ridiculous, worn out and just plain hopeless.'

Fast Forward to *not* having allowed a lot of illogical thought and irrational fear to lead you to uncontrollable panic, and from a place of calm, collected, logical, mindful thought you can very easily see yourself with no feelings of stupidity. You'll feel in control, and you won't be overwrought or fatigued. A far better scenario for you, and no doubt your companions/colleagues, who would have witnessed the alternative scenario, too.

So, Rewind, decide which it's to be. Play. And what you'll probably choose is to avoid a 'typical' panic attack by focusing on the outcome you want rather than assuming what might happen and fearing that outcome you so dread.

A child sufferer of panic attacks was brought to the clinic by her parents, and we were amazed at how easy it was to get her to engage with the therapy. Kids grasp it easier than anyone else.

Theft/Shoplifting

People who steal from shops are usually criticized by the general public for causing a hike in the cost of goods, because shopkeepers have to make up for their losses. Some of this shoplifting, though, is a manifestation of the recognized mental health problem, kleptomania. People find themselves compelled to steal relatively trivial items – such as the products stolen by several celebrities in the US and UK in recent years. Kleptomaniacs steal for similar trigger reasons to those with other behavioural compulsions – to gain control, or at least achieve a sense of control. Kleptomania often follows a series of traumas, and sufferers feel control has been taken away from them. Just the simple act of stealing a small item makes them feel empowered.

Some experts say that, even when there is temptation (wanting the goods) and self-justification (the belief the store can afford to lose the items), the ill-judged behaviour cannot happen without some kind of motivation.[7] In the case of shoplifting, that motivation could be the belief that there's no store security in view so there is no chance of being caught.

Given that pressing Pause can actually give a person a hugely increased sense of control in a very short time, it is likely that kleptomania would be another condition whose sufferers could benefit from PBT.

Even those prone to compulsive purchasing, rather than theft, might do well to Freeze Frame the moment before touching an item they really don't need. A study in the US suggested that merely holding a product made it more likely someone would buy the item, even if it were not something they needed in their household.[8] The researchers say the answer is to write a list, and prepare yourself before going shopping. We'd say that preparation could be to press Pause!

A PAUSE BUTTON MOMENT

I had a client called Ryan (not his real name), who was a cocaine addict. He lives in Spain and he came in with his wife. The deal she put to him was straightforward: if he used again she was going to leave him. She'd take the children, going to court if necessary to ensure she got custody, and he wouldn't see them again because of his addiction. Ryan's boss had already told him if he took any more time off work because of coke, he would lose his job, which meant he couldn't pay his mortgage and would lose his home. All these reasons were why he shouldn't use cocaine again.

So, say he went into a bar – 'coincidentally' the one where he usually met his coke mate, or his dealer – at that time; all he can think about is the next few moments, the high he'll get. He disregards everything he could lose; his life could be destroyed just because he's thinking of the next few seconds. But if he had the technique to think *beyond* the next few seconds, would he still go ahead and do it? Probably not.

The therapy's been developed so if you're right there in the bar, or wherever, in a sweat with tunnel vision, you hit your

Pause Button so you're physically paused. The thing, that choice, is still in front of you, but you've given yourself the time to take a deep breath. *Before* you have that first vodka shot, or even *after*, but *before* your mate says, 'Come on, let's just go to the toilet and have a couple of lines of coke, it'll make you feel better,' press the Pause Button and think – you're going to have 15 minutes of pleasure from those lines of coke, but what would the implications be? Let's run Fast Forward to tomorrow morning. Your eyes are shot, your wife knows you've used – what would the implications be for your marriage, your home, the future of your children, etc.? We talked it through and Ryan said, 'Yes, I know it's wrong, but I never think about it.'

I said, 'Well, I want you to use the Pause Button and actually *think* about it; now Rewind, and for once in your life stand up to this guy, this feeling, this emotion, this thought of pleasure and *don't* do it. Now Fast Forward to the following morning: your wife looks at you and says, "Great, darling, you didn't use" – and you get the children to school, you get to work on time, you plan a holiday for the family for next summer. Now, which scenario do you want?

'The pleasure of the first scenario is 15 minutes and nothing more – the cost is enormous. If you plan the other way you can work out the cost of not having it – well, maybe you're not so elated, maybe you can't stay up so late, but the benefits are going to be enormous.'

Ryan got on quite well with PBT. Has it worked all the time? No, it hasn't. Has it worked the majority of the time? Yes, but if Ryan and his wife were here now they'd both say that whatever has come out of it, for the first time in his life he's thinking about the consequences of his actions – and that's a good thing. That's an amazing thing!

A man Martin's counselled about the wide ramifications of cocaine use had been to university, done graphic design, and was capable of beautiful work. He'd used a bit of cocaine, then bought some and sold it to someone else. He got caught by the police and ended up with a criminal record for dealing. Within a calendar month his dream came true and he got offered a job in Los Angeles, but now he couldn't get a visa to go to the US because of his past behaviour.

If, on that day, that one event, he'd used PBT and thought about the consequences... Just think about it. *He* obviously didn't. He's got his degree, but now he can't use it in the way he'd always dreamed. What an amazing cost to him and his family.

Then there's the cost to the government of putting him through university; the lecturers; what his family had gone through to send him there; what his brothers and sisters had gone without. All lost in a heartbeat. If only he'd seen the consequences – would he have done the same thing?

This is never going to be a cure-all, the ultimate saviour, but it would just be good if we could get people to stage one, to start thinking about the future. Even if they don't make changes immediately, that first step of at least thinking about the future can be a major achievement.

Obesity

We are, of course, quite accustomed to hearing the usually flawed, illogical thought processes of those suffering from an apparent inability to shift excess weight.

Among the explanations given for eating to excess (i.e. when not hungry) are:

- Passing a baker's shop, smelling fresh buns and going in to buy goodies despite having just eaten (press Pause: Haven't you just eaten your lunch? Would you fill your car with fuel 20 minutes after refuelling?)

- Falling out with a friend and needing comfort (press Pause: Is there any logic in that? Food is to keep your body going; it does nothing for your head. You'll make up with your friend and feel worse for having eaten all that ice-cream when you didn't need it.)

- Eating bread, drinking wine, having a starter, main course and pudding at a restaurant... just because it's there on the menu (press Pause: Would you eat bread rolls *before* a three-course meal at home? Why pay for something you don't need? Don't you tend to eat them even if you're not hungry? Think again. What are the consequences of all this?)

- I've had one biscuit and ruined my efforts. I might as well eat the packet (press Pause: A lapse isn't a disaster. Just don't do it again. One biscuit won't make that much difference. Just learn from this.)

...and so on!

A 45-year-old woman called Mags came to us for help in addressing her literally growing problem with obesity. A chubby teenager who had played the class clown to make herself popular rather than deal with her overeating, she had snacked almost constantly, sometimes even taking loose change from her mother's purse to supplement her need for junk food.

Throughout her later teens she felt unable to express her love for style and fashion because, although she was still no more than a size 16, she believed her bulges would spoil the look of any outfit.

By her twenties, married and with two young children, she'd all but given up on believing she would ever be slimmer. She seemed incapable of stopping herself from feeding her growing appetite. She would feed the children, then eat their leftovers. Snack mid-morning on her favourite ginger nuts and coffee. Eat 'healthy' sandwiches for lunch... but topped off with her first half of a family-sized packet of crisps. Polish off several biscuits in the afternoon, each time she spotted that inviting packet. Then naturally hoover up the bits left in the pan after cooking the kids' supper.

All of which still left her plenty of room to eat a mammoth meal with hubby Greg – washed down with cola if she felt 'good', or rum and cola on her increasingly frequent bad days.

By the time she visited us, Mags was bursting out of her size 20 clothes and knew things were getting worse. She struggled to put on her tights and hated her husband seeing her undress or – heaven forbid – undressed. She puffed her way up any stairs and was dreading knowing the results of a recent sugar/cholesterol test requested by her doctor. She was heading for the dreaded fat and 50, and didn't like the thought.

Time for action.

We taught Mags that, rather than stuff her face, she should ask herself 'why?', and one way to help her do that was to press Pause whenever she felt she wanted to overeat. She learned that she should recognize hunger, and once she was in the PBT safe zone, no one could make her eat; she wouldn't die for lack of food, and it gave her time to look at the consequences of her actions.

If she ate those crisps? By using her Fast Forward, she could see that in 10 minutes, she would be beating herself up mentally, telling herself what a failure she was. Less than five minutes after that she would have eaten the whole packet, figuring nothing could make things worse. The next morning she would have been unable to play with the children at the school where she worked, her husband would have struggled to tell her that her 'bum didn't look big in that' and she'd have received the bad news from the surgery about her Type 2 diabetes diagnosis. Thankfully, though, she was able to Rewind, and Fast Forward again to facing that food and *not* eating. She would be able to see how proud she was; it might only be the first day but she'd be so chuffed with her control. As time went on she'd feel more and more confident and would work her way into those smaller sizes. Maybe even in time for whichever child's wedding was announced first! No rush, no panic. But she would be in control. Then she could Rewind, make her decision and come back to the present and choose whether or not to eat the food in front of her.

We taught her that one lapse isn't a failure, it's just another lesson learned.

Mags is still not at the size 12 she is hoping for, but she's healthier, happier, fitter and, what's more, the family food budget's been slimmed down, too!

Bed-wetting

An 11-year-old girl who, for just under a year, had been the victim of bullying at her new school began wetting the bed. Being bullied, at any age, can be a frightening experience. To then have the 'shame' of reverting to bed-wetting was a harrowing experience for her. She was introduced to PBT by her parents to help her overcome what everyone hoped would prove to be just a temporary problem.

It was what she *thought* about the bullying, though, that brought on the anxiety that caused the bed-wetting. It all started with a thought. She allowed the bullying to become much more than it actually was and blew it out of proportion in her mind.

She was encouraged to use the Pause Button to stop and think about how she was interpreting these other girls' actions. Why were they bullying her? Was it because *they* felt insecure? Because she was the new girl in the school and not yet part of their inner circle? Were they trying to get attention for themselves? Did they feel threatened by her?

After learning to use the PBT technique to stop and think about the consequences of her actions and her thoughts, what actually happened was that the time between the bed-wetting got greater and greater until she wasn't wetting the bed at all. Then she found that there were so many other areas of her life – even at 11 years of age – in which she could benefit from employing the technique.

Bulimia[9]

Susan had been suffering with bulimia for six years and she'd realized she had now reached a point in her life when she wanted to change her habits/addictions and work through her difficulties. The initial thing that needed to change was her relationship with food. Food, for Susan, was a coping technique, and life wouldn't change for her if she didn't address this.

Every time she wanted/needed to binge and/or vomit, she learned that using PBT could Pause the moment for a few seconds. She could then Fast Forward five minutes to see the ramifications and consequences of her actions. Doing this empowered her. It was the first time she'd been able to make a choice and take 'time out' to think about her actions. She was able to ask herself, did she really want to act on this need/want and feel the remorse and guilt? The option she now had was to see she could change things by taking a different route.

Bulimics frequently plan their day early on. If we could say, 'Stop at that point there, pause your thoughts and think about the implications of letting this thought process run on; think about throwing up, about the smell, think about what it's doing to your teeth and your oesophagus.' If we could get them to run through all the scenarios... what choice would they make?

Bulimics can binge for many reasons – stress, fatigue, boredom – but once the idea is there it takes on a life of its own. They possibly can't stop thinking about it and they plan – often standing in front of kitchen cabinets looking for things to eat; choosing which they want, whether sweet, savoury, treats, whatever – then eat, sometimes to what feels like bursting point, giving themselves 'enough' to purge.

Before they start they'll often eat a 'marker' – maybe a piece of red pepper – and they use it to see when they've got to the end of their purge.

The binge provides some kind of release. For some, bingeing even provides a feeling of extreme joy, followed by guilt, followed by the anger that follows the purge.

There's also secrecy – bulimics often hide the evidence of the bingeing from their family (wrappers, etc.), and most would recognize the 'stop, stop, stop, stop' repeating inside their head, too.

Once Susan was starting to use PBT, she was able to freeze time and see where her actions might lead. If she then pressed Rewind, came back to the present, and realized she hadn't followed through with this action, how would she feel?

Of course she then said she'd feel positive about the future, knowing there is another way to do things.

Even if she doesn't succeed every time, the one thing Susan has changed is that she is now able to take time to stop and consider that she has a choice. Stopping, visualizing and thinking are all part of this first step.

Every time Susan chooses to pause, think and change her action, and makes a choice not to binge/vomit, she says she feels *virtuous*, strong and positive. This 'feeds' her differently and empowers her. In Susan's case, she is in therapy too, and PBT is able to contribute to her process of understanding why she needed to 'cope' in this way in the first place.

How to Avoid Micro-managing: Using PBT in the Family

Bulimics' families provide a prime example of how those close to someone with an addictive or behavioural problem can actually exacerbate the issue with 'over care'.

They might make a big thing of sitting down together for family meals; make a point of watching what the sufferer eats; listen at the toilet door, anticipating a 'purge' session, and then clear up afterwards. All this does is reinforce the feeling that the sufferer can't deal with the problem themselves, that they don't have any self-control, need help, and cause problems for their family, etc. Not only does this lower their self-esteem still further, but every factor mentioned just serves to bring the issue to the forefront of the sufferer's mind.

The same pattern happens with other issues, including depression. Someone might 'kindly' ask, 'How are you feeling today, are you a bit down?' Well, actually, they may have been feeling fine *until that moment!*

Let's take a look at the importance of using PBT to help family members avoid having a negative effect on their loved one's attempts to change.

If you're with someone who's abusing one or other substance, and trying to come off it, and you're continually asking if they're using, checking their bedroom, sneaking a look at the texts on their mobile: how about thinking before you say or do anything? Press Pause next time you're about to leap in with both feet asking where they're going. Fast Forward. In the first scenario you *don't* check up on them – you leave them to live their life for that hour, that afternoon, without your minute intervention. How will that make them feel? Trusted? Believed in? Will it boost their confidence that those around them think they can make the change?

Rewind. Fast Forward, then take a peek down the other road. You badger them about where they're going. You grab a look at their mobile to see who they've been texting and receiving texts from. You insist you'll pick them up if they're not home by a certain time. What's the effect of that behaviour? Do they feel loved and cared for, or do they feel under the spotlight, under scrutiny, not trusted?

For that matter, how do *you* feel in these two scenarios? Do you feel like a calm, patient parent/sister/family member in the first and a nag in the second? Ever heard of micro-management?

Which do you think would most help their recovery? Or hinder it? Perhaps you should use PBT yourself to press Pause every time you feel yourself about to phone them to put pressure on them about their use/abuse?

Which is designed to make them aware of their substance of choice? Which is more likely to make them feel anxious, under pressure, insecure?

The same applies to bulimia, truancy, etc. So many − possibly all − of the problem behaviours we've identified would be dealt with better if the family took a loving step back from the brink of hassling!

If your child is playing truant from school and is now trying to stop, and you show a bit of trust and faith, maybe that would help them more than if you played the 'heavy'. Isn't it all about giving them the confidence that they can take control? And if you demonstrate you believe in them, that's one step nearer achieving the end you all want.

Listen to a couple of other thoughts from the 'front line':

'I'm really trying to cut down on my drinking, but every time I take the dog out for a walk, my wife checks to see if I've got any money on me to go to the bar for a drink − I hadn't even thought about that, but she's always on about drink and she keeps putting it at the front of my mind.'

'I hadn't even thought about skipping school, but Mum insists on walking to school with me; she even says she knows I'm going to play truant... I wouldn't have thought of it if she didn't go on about it.'

So, we've spoken in some detail about thought processes. But if you're blunt with yourself, could you really say you've ever *thought* about any of these actions at all? No, we thought not − or at least, if you did, it wasn't very much of a thought before you just went ahead and did it anyway. Now you know, so you need to spot those illogical thoughts as they come up. You know you need to identify when you're planning to carry out your negative actions. Now you know you have the *choice* to think – about what you're doing, but more importantly, the consequences of what you're doing. You've given yourself time by pressing Pause.

Yes we, and more importantly you, know at the end of the day you might still go on to do your 'thing', but you can chalk up a major success for thinking in more detail than you've ever done before. You've considered the consequences thoroughly, possibly for the first time ever. You now have a precedent – you can do it again, and next time you might choose differently. You certainly have the tools to think things through more comprehensively, and, despite the fact that you 'messed up' this time (we know you'll see it this way, so why beat about the bush?!), you are one major step nearer to developing confidence in your own ability *not* to slip up another time.

In the case of addictive behaviours, it's most likely that the model of change (the process described earlier, from not knowing what you don't know, through to something like second nature) happens without anyone necessarily identifying it. So the addict doesn't even know they have a problem; knows the problem exists but not how significant it is; knows how bad the problem is and wants to change; starts changing and, ultimately, the hope would be that the habit would be eradicated or replaced by a better, alcohol- or drug- or whatever-free Pause Button habit!

That virtuous circle again.

An ancient Asian proverb expresses a different, maybe more user-friendly perspective to Maslow's Learning Cycle concept:

He who knows not, and knows not that he knows not,
is a fool – shun him,
He who knows not, and knows that he knows not,
is ignorant – teach him,

He who knows, and knows not that he knows,
is asleep – wake him,
But he who knows, and knows that he knows,
is a wise man – follow him.

Consequences are direct results that occur after a decision has been made.

There are two types of consequences we should consider: reinforcements and punishments.

With reinforcement as a consequence, your behaviour increases, and with punishment as a consequence, your behaviour decreases.

Pause Button Therapy is a rehearsal of the consequences.

A PAUSE BUTTON MOMENT

Fiona Graham writes:

If only! When writing a book about preventing the bad consequences of foolish, short-sighted, avoidable, knee-jerk, mindless decisions, you'd think the first thing you'd make a point of integrating into your life would be to do what you know will work. What you're writing about. Press Pause at every possible eventuality. Not least to avoid having to write an embarrassing addendum containing an admission as enormous as this!

One Thursday in February 2012 I effectively lost this book by not pressing Pause. Well, my only two pre-publication e-copies, that is. The pen drive I usually work from and –

worse – the two-month-old Toshiba laptop containing my only version saved to hard drive. Aaaaaaagh! How?

I know the sequence well enough I could say it in my sleep. How did it get circumvented so stupidly, costing me dear in grey hairs, stress and no small amount of money in replacement(s)?

Simple. I didn't press Pause. Outside the Nissan dealership where I take my car for servicing, when transferring my shopping from the courtesy car to my own, I essentially ignored Martin's, Marion's and even my own mantra of advice. I left the bags – and the laptop bag (also containing the expensive mini-tape machine beloved of reporters) – on the pavement for a few minutes while I dealt with the bill.

Yes, I know.

To provide an attempt at self-defence, I had my reasons: sparsely populated industrial estate, last appointment of the evening, no one in sight, son messing around nearby, staff in and out of the door some 18 inches away dealing with the one other remaining customer.

So at any point did I question my own decision to surround the laptop with supermarket bags and leave it outside? If I'm honest, maybe just fleetingly, yes. And it was there, then, at that brief moment of doubt, that actually using PBT would have changed the course of the next several weeks.

If I'd thought about what I would be able to do or not do if I didn't have file 'USB PBT' and file 'USB research' and all the others, and my camera memory card and the USB stick with the contents of my old redundant laptop, just picked up from the computer shop earlier the same day.

What would I actually do? What would it mean to my life and those of my family? My elder son would have to scout around for a copy set of his beloved wedding photos. I'd have lost forever the first photos of my younger son playing rugby. The photos I took of all three of my children at the wedding – daughter resplendent as a bridesmaid for the first time.

I'd have to wave goodbye to another £600 in laptop equipment, software, anti-virals, etc. All this on top of making umpteen visits to file a theft report at the police station 35 miles away.

And Martin and Marion? How to explain the ridiculous turn of events leading to the loss of their second book?

So… All those thoughts and more should have crossed my mind as I imagined, PBT-style, the consequences of putting my laptop on the pavement rather than in the garage office a few feet away. But they didn't.

'Why?' is a very good question, and I suspect the only honest answer is because I haven't taken my own medicine and practised the PBT sequence in everyday life anywhere near enough. If I had I would probably have seen that glint of doubt and Paused to consider the possible ramifications.

The lesson to learn from this is, yes, as has been said earlier on, we're all fallible. No, it doesn't mean PBT is useless – it means that on that occasion I was somewhat useless myself. Please learn from this. I have.

Oh, and the postscript to this? Martin pointed out that, at his request, I had saved a copy of the book to the hard drive at the clinic. PBT clearly worked for us, thanks to him!

A PAUSE BUTTON MOMENT

No matter how much Lilly tried, she could not get any more things in her wardrobe; it was bursting at the seams. Shopping, finding bargains and bidding online were her favourite pastime. Not rich, she just puts everything on plastic… and four years of that have left her with two major problems: lack of cupboard space, and a bad credit rating.

Lilly heard of PBT whilst online. Using it means she can Pause when she fancies buying yet one more item. She imagines a flat full of unworn clothes, a life spent paying back her debt, a life never being able to afford a holiday. Her second Fast Forward allows her to see how her life could be: a nice selection of clothes to wear, the rest sold on an online auction site to help pay off her debts, more money in her bank at the end of each month. In fact, a real future without constant money worries. Returning to the present, she can make her choice of what to do, and press Play.

IN THIS CHAPTER YOU'VE LEARNED:

- Really get to understand what sets you off…
- Know your triggers.
- Visualizing consequences.

---

*Pause * Think * Decide * Act*

PART 4
PBT POTENTIAL

HOW PBT COULD HELP CUT GOVERNMENT SPENDING

'Choices are the hinges of destiny.'
PYTHAGORAS

We have long believed that pressing Pause would be an incredibly efficient way to reduce repeat offending. Figures released at the end of 2011[1] show just how important this could be for UK prisons and prison expenditure. The Police National Computer issued statistics showing that one-fifth of the burglaries in 2010 were committed by criminals freed on bail. That amounts to one offence about every five minutes.

Furthermore, suspects already on bail for other offences committed over 140,000 crimes resulting in a caution, conviction, warning or reprimand. The figure could well be even higher, because figures aren't recorded in a consistent way. Bail suspects were responsible for 707 sexual offences, 11 per cent of violent offences (including murders and serious assaults) and almost 1 in 10 drug offences.

To sum up, 'bail bandits' committed about 1 in 10 of all crimes detected in 2010. What do you suppose the cost of all this offending and re-offending adds up to? On top of the price per prisoner per year, there's the cost of court time, social workers, probation officers, police hours and so on.

Some experts working within Victim Support[2] in the UK are recognizing the potential benefits of 'encouraging' (perhaps *insisting* would be a better word) offenders to look thoroughly at the effects of their offences.

That way of looking at the problem ties in perfectly with Martin's belief that PBT provides a distinctly cost-effective way of reducing not only re-offending, but the attendant costs.

What if every prisoner, every young offender, were either given this book or required to complete a course in PBT before being released? They'd then have the tools to change their own future for the better. Whenever they were about to go out with the gang of bad lads they used to hang around with, they'd be able to press Pause and look at the consequences of that choice.

Pause. What's better for you? To go out, drink too much, maybe steal a car, buy some drugs, get caught and end up going through the justice system again, or (Rewind) Play again: tell those minor criminals you've had it with that lifestyle, ignore their badgering and stay home with your family for a change, catching up on old times? Not a hard choice when you look at the effects on everyone around you…

With PBT input from therapists or social workers, we're sure the benefits would be even greater and could make a serious impact on re-offending.

The cost of keeping someone in a Young Offender Institution (YOI) or prison averaged around £40,000 per inmate in 2010.[3] Even a 5 or 10 per cent reduction in re-offending would, therefore, provide significant cost benefits.

The cost of introducing PBT (or this book) is small in terms of the combined police, court, prison and re-offence bill. With a success rate of even 50 per cent, it would save thousands, possibly hundreds of thousands of pounds. We'd need only a small change in the overall rate of re-offending to result in millions of public pounds saved.

The savings aren't just financial, either. What about saving upset to people's family and extended family? What about the victims and their families? What about the parents whose kid has been in jail and comes out and re-offends; what it does to them and their outlook on life, and how it affects their other children?

If the guy who has been let out had been given this chance, had been taught the PBT technique before leaving jail, he may actually have started to think of the consequences of his actions, of what he was about to do. If he could see and feel what it was like to know he was going back to jail, surely he would think harder about his actions?

Maybe we should introduce PBT within the prison network so prisoners have the training *before* they're released?

Or perhaps magistrates and judges should use PBT as part of their sentencing menu? Is putting kids in jail, immersing them in a cauldron of people who are drug users, pimps, thieves and violent criminals, the best use of various governments' money, time and effort?

It's not just about the cost of police and court time – other expenses could include years of unemployment benefit if ex-offenders can't then get a job. What's the total cost of all that to the taxpayer? It may even dwarf the police and prison costs.

One of the biggest budgets for any government is that of health care. Spending on obesity-related problems, alcohol-related problems, anti-depressants and diabetes all adds up to huge sums in the UK alone.

In 2010 the spend on slimming pills was approaching £50 million, and the total cost of obesity-related illness is estimated to rise by up to £2 billion per year by 2030.[4] By 2011, anti-depressant use had risen by over 25 per cent in England over the previous three years.[5] The number of prescriptions for anti-depressants increased by 28 per cent, from 34 million in 2007–2008 to 43.4 million in 2010–2011, according to the NHS Information Centre. The cost of treating depression is running at over £520 million per year. These are extraordinary figures for what, we'd argue, are sticking plaster treatments.

Martin feels that sometimes it seems there are many doctors who don't have time to treat *causes* – they treat *symptoms*. It's what Gay Jones has called 'the sticking plaster mentality', which does not address or think about *why* a person is the way they are. Martin knew someone who was given anti-depressants 'for six weeks' – 17 years on, they're still taking them. We're all paying for this, through income tax.

> *'There are very few doctors who treat causes;*
> *they treat symptoms.'*
> **MARTIN SHIRRAN**

Doctors have about seven minutes with each patient.[6] They haven't got enough time to find out about people. If someone comes in saying they're drinking a bottle of vodka a day, the last thing you do is take the vodka away. You find out why they're doing it. If it's because the husband's coming home and kicking hell out of her, then the vodka's not the underlying problem. Sort out the cause and the symptoms will disappear. The doctors don't have time for that. They can hand out drugs, but they're never going to find out why this patient is drinking a bottle of vodka a day. Why does she come to the surgery crying and depressed? When she comes off the anti-depressants in six weeks' time, that situation is still there and she'll be back, crying about it. She'll have to have another prescription. But that's treating the symptom, not the cause. Doctors just don't have the time to get to the root of the matter.

Maybe the first place for doctors to use PBT would be on themselves – think, 'If I write out this prescription for this person, where will she be in a month's time? Will she be dependent on the pills? Am I really doing the best for this person?'

This is one of the ways in which Martin believes PBT could be such a cost-effective, simple tool within the NHS. What if, before doling out Prozac, there was the option of giving patients 20 minutes with the Practice Nurse to learn PBT?

Gay Jones feels that doctors, ultimately, will be on side. 'It's about recognizing their sensitivities,' she explains. 'At the moment they've been accused of overprescribing, and on top of that they might have to be saving money. So we have to be very clear in our evidence.'

There is new research suggesting that newly diagnosed Type 2 diabetes is reversible.[7] Putting PBT in medical centres or hospitals, with discharge nurses, would be an amazing back-up plan, according to both Martin and Gay.

Gay believes doctors do want solutions, because they're given hopeless targets. Type 2 diabetes (and also other conditions and problems) is a *symptom* of what is happening rather than the cause. Maybe we should get the person leaving hospital with a diagnosis of diabetes to see the benefit of making lifestyle changes now... benefits not only to himself, but to his family.

Martin's list is extensive: he feels PBT could also be the subject of in-house training in psychiatric hospitals, and helping nurses assist with chronic and acute illness. He makes the point that patients dealing with liver or kidney transplants will cost the NHS large sums, but many may well have contributed to their own ill-health by lifestyle choices. Addressing substance use and abuse, he asserts, could well slash these expenses.

Road rage, too – have you ever considered the costs of that? If there's a traffic accident as a result, a motorway may have to be shut and police called out. Injuries will involve the health service(s). Other motorists' days will be disrupted. A large ripple effect that could have been prevented if the person with the anger problem had learned to press Pause.

PBT in the driving test might help new drivers, particularly young people. What if we got them to actually Pause and think what they are about to do? Maybe they would learn that going a half-step further and putting their imagination into slow motion, thinking through every last traffic sign, pedestrian, junction and so on, would give them better clarity of vision about what's happening around them. Not unlike advanced police driver training!

One visit to A&E costs the NHS around £68 for assessment alone. A test could add £120-plus.[8] Self-harm cases could total £400 each, from arrival to eventual discharge. Not a lot in isolation, but consider the numbers when you look at repeat visits. It's better to address the cause rather than spend repeated sums of money on the symptom.

The cost of treating someone with bulimia, or another eating disorder, can be as much as £45,000, according to the

Eating Disorders Association (EDA).[9] A three-month in-patient course on the NHS could reach £25,000 – and because of the costs involved, many areas have no in-patient provision.

People with eating disorders can cost the NHS twice or three times over, though, because they can suffer side-effects such as infertility, osteoporosis, heart failure, kidney and dental problems.[10]

Quite a saving, then, if using a PBT method reduces the effect of the disorder or, better still, completely cures it.

It is calculated that to implement UK guidelines on treating Obsessive Compulsive Disorder (OCD) will cost between £29 million and £75 million simply for adults.[11]

In England, smoking was calculated to have cost the NHS around £5 billion in 2005/06.[12] Even stop-smoking treatment, which cost £84 million in 2009,[13] would seem cost-effective against a problem of that scale.

And the overall rate of smokers has remained fairly stable, at about 27 per cent of the adult population. So no major success story.

How about trying to press Pause instead? Look at the consequences, then take control, take responsibility. And save the public health budget!

> *'PBT almost comes around from behind you like peripheral vision – where couldn't you use it.'*
> **MARTIN SHIRRAN**

PBT in the Commercial Sector

Such was the initial workload involved in refining the PBT technique that it took a while for its full potential to become clear.

But once Martin was on a roll with ideas, he realized he wasn't sure at all what the limits were. Or, more accurately, he was sure the limits were... well, nigh on limitless! Addictions, behaviours, adults, children, health services, education – all morphed into part of the PBT stable. Probably the only one we haven't yet touched on is the use of the system within commerce.

Where better to employ a 'think first, then act' type methodology than in customer service? Don't most companies, pretty much regardless of what line of business they're in, have a public face that might better serve its client base if the PBT approach was tried and tested rather than left up to individuals' mood and temper on the day?

When you start to analyze customer service, again, the list is extensive. Receptionists in hotels, restaurants, hospitals, doctors' surgeries, staff in supermarkets, on customer service desks, parking wardens, waiters, waitresses, airline cabin crew, medical staff, council workers, drivers and attendants on public transport, carers...

But it doesn't stop there. Sales and marketing. Public Relations. Which jobs are the most stressful? Add those to the list!

A 'for instance'. If a customer says to a salesman, 'Give me your best price *now*', instead of the salesman going straight to the figure for his best deal, he presses Pause and remembers what will give him the best consequence. He holds something back to use later on in a different way. So he doesn't come back with his best price, does he?! He can use Pause to stop a conversation and think about different ways of approaching it.

'The right word may be effective, but no word was ever as effective as a rightly timed pause.'
MARK TWAIN

Top salespeople, despite popular belief, tend to be listeners rather than talkers.

Maybe this is about how the sales manager incentivizes his staff. Does he use a Pause? Does he think about what he can do and what he can't? About his staff's family and children? You've got to wind it back; think it through really thoroughly. See all the consequences.

Another scenario. Say the person behind the counter in a cafeteria is as grumpy as sin. How likely are they to get any tips? How about using the Pause button to consider the effect on their customers? Is the waitress with the smile and the pleasant chat likely to get the best tip, or will it be the sullen, silent one? What do you think? It might simply be that the pleasant one will have the happier customer. That would be quite a result!

A hotel receptionist? It's the same story, really. Someone comes and checks in, and later on says, 'This room's not right, I need disabled facilities, it's too noisy, we're right next to a lift'. There are two ways the receptionist can handle it. She just needs to think about the consequences for her promotion prospects, her job security, the guest reporting her to a senior member of staff, that person coming back (or not) for a repeat booking, improving the profitability of the company and how that affects her in the long term, her pension, etc. She needs to think about the consequences before she opens her mouth and gets shirty with the customer.

Anyone in customer service will have encountered anger and frustration welling up. Anyone on a customer service desk, on a customer service telephone line, will know the difficult conversation well enough. If you feel yourself filling up with anxiety and anger, pressing Pause will give you options.

Pressing Pause will help you see the best moment to ask questions to clarify what the person is hoping to obtain/achieve.

Fast Forwarding to see the good and bad potential outcomes will allow you to make an informed choice as to how to act or react. Not to mention that it will give you (and your customer) the perfect opportunity simply to breathe!

Take a look at airlines, utility companies and the like. How many people actually use empathy and put themselves in their clients' place? All you get is this switchboard, that switchboard; you're left hanging… is it never thought through? There's no human contact. If only they could press Pause and think, 'What's the worst situation a customer could be in?'

On more than one occasion while on a flight, Martin (and surely he's not the only one) has spotted 'situations' between cabin crew and passengers. Sat there and watched the whole thing develop. He says sometimes it gets very nasty. If the crew had been given the opportunity to take time to assess the situation – maybe the passenger is just terrified of flying, or their mother's just died, or they've just been told their wife wants a divorce. Normally cabin crew are very good at assessment, but with 130 passengers, often many more, they haven't got time to study everybody. PBT could help focus them on this 'assessment' element of their job.

In any customer service situation – it doesn't matter if we're talking telesales, face to face, on flights, in retail – we just want the person to press Pause and stop and think about the consequences of their actions. Use a bit of empathy; think through how this is going to pan out, how this is going to develop. If this customer leaves here satisfied, and they therefore come back and purchase again, and tell their friends how well they were looked after, will it improve my chances of long-term employment. Will it have a positive impact for my family and children in the future, or not?

A PAUSE BUTTON MOMENT

A man (we'll call him Juan) spots that a client has left his mobile in the car he's left at Juan's out-of-the-way but cheap little Park-and-Ride car park near a cruise terminal. The customer is already thoroughly wound up at the prospect of having to organize a taxi to fetch the vital business phone, concerned about the ship leaving port, stressed before he's even started his holiday.

Mr X, the customer, takes a deep breath, expecting hassle, and phones Juan. Juan, nice as pie, points out he's seen the phone, recovered it from the car, and will send it with the next scheduled minibus to the port, within 10 minutes.

Consequences? Well, clearly Mr X is de-stressed, happy and ready for his cruise. More than that, though, within the next few months he will have recommended that funny little car park to anyone he can. He will have passed Juan quite a tidy sum in extra business. That thoughtfulness cost Juan nothing. The minibus was going to the docks anyway. That was customer service. With consequences.

You need to ask yourself: 'How important is the way I handle this woman who's standing here complaining about those sunglasses she bought yesterday?' The easy thing to do would be to get rid of her any way I can. She's just one customer. But she has a voice. She talks to other people. The effects ripple down. People have to think about the consequences of their actions. You can be rude to one person, but the effect on your job, your family, your children, could be catastrophic.

People going for a job interview – do they stop and use empathy? What is the interviewer looking for? How have I got to behave to impress them? What can I say that would improve my chances? Let me press Pause and think. There are two ways of going in – dressed like *this*, with *this* attitude and get *this* outcome, or go in dressed like *that* with a different attitude and get a different outcome. Would it work in recruitment and get people their first job?

Martin firmly believes the ethos for any company should start at the top and gravitate downwards. So, how the chief executive reacts to her PA is passed down, and the effect will be felt in the entire company; whole companies could benefit from establishing a Pause Button ethos.

In truth, we'd expect that most company chairs have already 'got it'. But we know from some news stories that there've been too many foul-ups.

A PAUSE BUTTON MOMENT

It didn't make any difference how many times Shelley tried to stop, when her kids annoyed her she resorted to yelling. Worse still, that sometimes morphed into smacking, despite her best intentions. Only eight and six years old, they didn't deserve to have a mum shouting at them so often. She knew it; she just didn't seem able to do much about it. Occasionally she'd hold back the shouting, but it usually happened one way or the other. Tears all round. Until Shelley spotted a mention of PBT and the Pause technique online.

Thinking nothing could really hurt, she practised 'zapping' herself with her imaginary remote control, pressing her thumb and forefinger just like using the real thing. Once she started recognizing when she was likely to lose control, she learned to press Pause without delay. She was able to take herself forward to visualize how she'd feel having 'lost it' once more. To see the children's tear-stained faces, hear their sobbing. To recognize that ghastly empty feeling of being a useless, out-of-control parent. But she could also Rewind, and Fast Forward again to see what would happen if she held her tongue, spoke calmly to tell the children what she expected and why she expected it. To tell them of the consequences if they didn't behave. What a turn-up for the books – Shelley telling her kids about consequences! So, once she had the time to really consider the two options, she could then come back to the present, make her decision and press Play. And get on with a more disciplined, calmer future for the whole family.

IN THIS CHAPTER YOU'VE LEARNED:

- Should courts hand down PBT Orders?
- Making customer service a service to the customer.
- Visualizing consequences.

*Pause * Think * Decide * Act*

10

USING PBT WITH CHILDREN AND YOUNG PEOPLE – GAY JONES, MA, BEd (Hons)

*L*atterly Project Director of an Education Action Zone, Gay Jones has specialized in school improvement and change for over 20 years. She has been involved in education since the mid-1980s, when she was a teacher in Birmingham, UK. Her passion has been to maximize achievements and develop programmes that engage and motivate, among others being those aiming to raise standards in writing and numeracy, transform learning environments, improve family involvement and implement emotional literacy strategies.

A trained NLP Practitioner and Energy for Life Coach, she has been enthusiastic about PBT from the outset and came on board with PBT International within months of the start of planning this book.

In 2011, Gay developed PBT for use with children and young people in schools and other institutional settings. She has created support materials and training sessions for teaching and support staff, children and parents.

Gay has written this chapter to explain the processes that underlie PBT. Teachers, parents and other childcare workers will benefit from becoming familiar with how brain development and psychology influence how we use PBT with young people. She also talks about her belief in PBT, and includes quotes from some of the people involved in 'live trials' in schools. She gives a description of how to present PBT to children and young people for daily use.

Teachers, parents and specialist staff have said that the PBT system is so simple they initially found it hard to believe just how effective it is. The impact of PBT has been proven with children, teenagers and adults, and it is surprising to find just how easily the technique makes behaviour change. With so much evidence of classroom disruption and loss of teaching time due to dealing with discipline issues prevalent in the UK, the time is right to introduce PBT – simple, radically different and unique.

In this chapter you will:

- discover how PBT creates new habits
- learn simple and powerful techniques to make better choices
- find out how to make the new learning 'stick'
- read first-hand accounts of lives changed by PBT.

'We've been working hard on helping him to calm down and he had started to; the PBT wristband has given him that extra bit of a push. It's just a piece of rubber but the effects are really surprising!'
SIOBHAN, MOTHER OF A 10-YEAR-OLD

Whether you want to reduce anger, prevent aggressive reactions, become more confident or be happier with your behaviour choices, PBT is exactly what you have been looking for. Whether you are a parent, a child, a teenager or a professional committed to changing lives through your interventions – you will find that PBT can be 'the difference that makes the difference'.[1]

PBT is now available to help children change their futures. In addition to the positive effects on children's lives, schools piloting PBT have identified just how much time and resources can be saved – and how quickly.

I'll be revealing easy strategies for facilitating behaviour change in children and young people. I'll share some tried-and-tested techniques that can be used immediately to make users feel happier, more in control – now and into the future.

Throughout this chapter I will share with you the stories of ordinary children with problems who have already achieved extraordinary results using this simple technique.

Behaviour modification and management has increasingly become a major focus for many schools over the past 50 years. Talking to teachers, they say that there have been too many initiatives resulting in too little change for too many children. Society sends contradictory messages to both parents and professionals, leaving the recipients exhausted and often unclear about what they 'should' be doing.

Do they ignore bad behaviour, impose sanctions or sit them on the naughty step? Some strategies work, but what is needed is something that takes the confusion out of the situation. Could the answer be something as simple as getting the child's brain on board? I believe the answer is yes!

Every time a behaviour strategy fails, every time a child repeats a behaviour, the more that child is convinced they have no other choices – that they are stuck. Their choices become more limited with every repeat of the behaviour and the more disheartened they become. They may be very aware of this defeated cycle, or they may not notice – the habitual response is so ingrained, they never realize they have other choices. The consequences become more and more severe – the repercussions for the child and society as a whole become ever more costly.

PBT helps break this cycle, by putting the choice, and the responsibility, into the child's own hands – literally.

To misquote Einstein... 'If we keep doing the same thing in the same way – why are we so surprised when we get the same results?'

The 'marshmallow' experiment conducted by Walter Mischel at Stanford University, US, in 1972 was designed to measure the ability to defer gratification. Nursery children were brought into a room, one at a time. They were given one marshmallow, and told they were allowed to eat it immediately, but if they could wait 15 minutes without eating it, they'd be given a second marshmallow, and could eat both. Seventy per cent of the children ate the marshmallow right away. Only 30 per cent could wait the full 15 minutes to get the second marshmallow. This experiment has been repeated in the intervening years, and the ratio stays the same.

Mischel later discovered that the children who were able to wait, not eat the first marshmallow and receive the reward of a second marshmallow, were more likely to succeed socially and academically. The ability to defer gratification produces children who are happier generally, and is also an indicator of future success. Those who didn't wait for the second marshmallow later showed less academic success, poorer relationships with peers and adults, and a greater likelihood of involvement in anti-social behaviour.

Pause Button Therapy uses visualization and imagining ourselves in future situations to train/encourage/demonstrate to children (and adults) in order to learn the benefits of anticipating the consequences of our choices – whether that's about getting a second marshmallow or more life-changing matters!

Imagination and Fantasy

Many children live in a fantasy world. 'So what?' you might say. 'Children have always lived in a fantasy world – I remember when I was a child…' However, their fantasy life today is often provided externally through DVDs, video games, virtual reality scenarios – most often in a solitary fashion with little physical movement. In the past, fantasy might have been stimulated by books, films or television, but the acting out was instigated by the children themselves – often in groups.

A 2009 University of Bristol study found that those children who spent more than two hours per day watching TV or using a computer were at an increased risk of psychological difficulties.

ChildWise research agency data for 2012 states that the overall time spent in front of screens by five- to 16-year-olds in Britain is nearly six hours a day.

Every newspaper we read has articles about children and young people who break society's rules. They suffer serious consequences through not thinking before they act. These problems include involvement in crime, rioting and poor behaviour preventing learning. The causes of poor behaviour are diverse.

They range from inadequate nutrition, unsound parenting styles, lack of sleep, incomplete brain development[2] and a tendency to be present-oriented in terms of time perspective.

There are many studies that detail the psychological, nutritional and physical needs of children in order to create a healthy, well-rounded child. There is documented evidence that shows how schools and other settings are more successful in their interventions when they work together with families and carers.[3]

Whilst PBT cannot change personal circumstances, it can provide a range of skills that will bring lifelong benefits.

What if there were a simple to use, effective and low-cost solution? What if children could change their behaviour just by pressing Pause and using their imagination to change how they react? This solution already exists in the form of Pause Button Therapy.

The hindsight question:
If you knew then what you know now,
what would you have done differently?

The Real Cost of Poor Behaviour

The first report of the House of Commons Education Committee refers to an international OECD (Organization for Economic Co-operation and Development) survey which suggests that as much as 30 per cent of teaching time can be lost to poor classroom behaviour.[4]

Poor behaviour also has an impact on learning. According to a survey of NASUWT (the UK's largest teaching union) members in March 2009, low-level disruption was leading to the loss of an average of 30 minutes' teaching time per teacher per day – that's 2.5 hours per teacher per week.

Using average salary costs for one teacher and one member of support staff, the total cost in lost staff time because of poor behaviour could be between £15,000 and £28,000 a year for a small primary school.

At a time when we are facing severe financial restraint in the UK, this seems outrageous.

Getting Our Brains to Work for Us

The most important bits of the brain in PBT terms are the *neurons* – we have around 100 billion of them, and each has over 60,000 connections with other brain cells. Neurons are the connecting links between the world we see and the world we act on. They carry information and generate electricity that jumps gaps and allows the release of chemical transmitters that can forge new information routes called neuro-nets, or neural pathways. The stronger the electrical excitement, the more chemicals are released and the more deeply embedded are the new routes.

David A. Sousa, international educational neuroscience consultant, tells of the effects of two chemicals: endorphins and dopamine. Dr Sousa writes of ways to develop improved learning strategies using current brain research. When a learning situation is a positive one, these chemicals become activated. Endorphins make the student happy or euphoric, and dopamine stimulates the part of the brain that makes a person remain attentive and more likely to remember what is being taught.

In negative situations (or a negative learning experience), the hormone cortisol will enter the bloodstream, putting the brain into survival mode and shifting attention away from learning so it can deal with the stress. That memory will be imprinted to make negative learning experiences even less likely to be successful.

We use PBT as a tool to access emotions and stimulate neuron activity, by creating high levels of engagement and interest, which create chemical excitement, which in turn releases more chemicals. This creates a positive effect, pleasant feelings, and emotions that encourage the body to re-experience the results repeatedly, until a new behaviour or highway is created and the road that led to the unwanted behaviour becomes overgrown through lack of use.

Children may have developed habits and ways of behaving that cause concern, but they can be taught techniques that counteract their current responses. Brain plasticity reference research suggests that once the brain is shown how to think differently, new habits or neural pathways can be formed and maintained through practice. Children do not have to believe that this will work, nor understand the underlying theories. They only have to be willing to use the PBT technique. They then need to practise the process repeatedly; this will help them to make changes to their behavioural choices.

When practising PBT, there are certain factors that will help:

- paying attention to how you feel
- trusting yourself
- knowing that you have a complex, creative brain that will produce plenty of alternative choices once you ask it to.

The person trying out PBT needs to have a desire to undertake, and stick with, the process. I'm not suggesting that PBT is a miracle cure – it does require repetition and a desire to change – but the results can feel miraculous to the child, the parents and the teaching staff who are experiencing the benefits.

Every time we use the PBT method, we are increasing the likelihood of creating long-term change. We are forging new 'habit pathways' or neuro-nets. The more we use the method, the more successes we enjoy, and the deeper the behaviour gets ingrained – soon, a new habit pathway is formed, and we will tend to go that route as a matter of course.

It is important that the user understands that successful behaviour change is not a smooth process; it takes time and effort. We should encourage them to think of behaviour change as a long process in which they build on each small success, learning from any setbacks.

Successful behaviour change is rarely a smooth process

There may be setbacks on your path to successful behaviour change

Remember: the mind doesn't distinguish between reality, memory and thoughts, so even doing this exercise in your imagination will have an effect on your behaviour.

'Before I started using my PBT wristband, I was in trouble every day. I used to get into fights. I never received any rewards – or if I did, they got taken away again the next time I was naughty. My mum was fed up of the school phoning her to have meetings about me. I was fed up and couldn't seem to be good. I'd try but then do the same things again.

The teachers asked me if I'd like to try PBT and I thought, "Why not?" I was fed up of being in trouble all the time and not enjoying school. I was also arguing with my brother all the time.

Once I started using the band every day, I was amazed at how easy it was to think about what would happen if I did this or that. I soon realized that I could pause and think.

I now really enjoy school. I don't fight every day. I find that I'm happier and people are playing with me now I'm not angry all the time. My mum hasn't had to come in to school and the only phone call she had was the head teacher telling her how much my behaviour has improved!'

JOE, AGED 11

Learning to Be Responsible for Our Actions

Many of us have been programmed to think that we have to keep repeating our mistakes and poor choices. We tend to go down the road we know, but that doesn't mean we can't try a new route.

Maslow's Learning Cycle (outlined earlier, in Chapter 8) describes how we learn something new. We move through these stages:

Unconscious Incompetence	Conscious Incompetence	Conscious Competence	Unconscious Competence
We don't know that we lack a skill.	We become aware of lacking a skill that others may have.	We've learned a new skill, but we have to think about how we accomplish it.	We use the skill automatically and don't have to think about it.

However, we do need to practise each step until we have created a new habit, route or pathway; until we know it so well that it becomes our path of choice more often than not.

These three words are all you need to remember:

Practise, Practise, Practise

Try This Experiment and See How It Feels

Remember a time when you made a decision without thinking it through. Remember any negative impacts.

How did you feel? What were the consequences on your relationships? What was the impact on your life?

Now take a few moments to imagine using PBT to easily change your behaviour:

- Pause.
- Fast Forward to visualize the negative consequences of making a bad choice of action. Make it vivid and real.
- Rewind back to the present.
- Make any adjustments – 'tweak' to fit.
- Rewind back to the present once you are happy.
- Play – live that behaviour.

How good does this feel?

What are you choosing to do differently?

What will your life be like when you have changed your behaviour?

Believe It or Not?

Don't give yourself a hard time if you make better choices 20 per cent, 40 per cent or 60 per cent of the time at first. We all have a tendency to expect immediate results. You *will* achieve results, and the more times you make a better choice and experience positive consequences, the more you will be inspired to make better choices. This will change your life and you will be less and less likely to react to out-of-date external triggers.

The more often you make conscious, different choices, the more often you will creatively use PBT to change your behaviour. Improvement and new habits will naturally follow. Remember the Pareto principle, otherwise known as the 80/20 per cent rule. Have a look at the behaviours that make you feel good or less good. You might feel as if a behaviour you engage in for 20 per cent of your time impacts on the other 80 per cent to leave you feeling very negative. The aim is to swap these percentages around.

If you can behave in a way that makes you feel good for 80 per cent of the time, the other 20 per cent becomes less important and matters less.

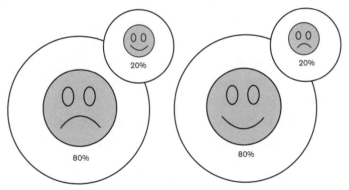

The 80/20 per cent rule

'At first it felt like I had to use PBT all the time. I realized how often I reacted aggressively to being pushed, people saying things, fighting at playtimes. I'm calmer and I don't just react. I think.'
HANNAH, AGED 11

Rewards

Human beings generally want to feel that any choice will bring a reward – this may be positive and beneficial, or negative and to our detriment. PBT helps us to choose a path that brings more positive rewards and reactions from both inside ourselves and from others.

There may have been many times when a child has gone through the behaviour process – a behaviour occurs and the school system kicks in; which may involve discussions, sanctions, recording, reflecting, apologizing and often promising not to repeat the behaviour. Everyone involved has their own emotions, which may include frustration, sorrow, remorse, anger – very few positive feelings result from such incidents that are repeated daily in schools worldwide.

However, this is continual proof that bad habits and behaviours rarely respond to promises to change. What needs to change is the mind – or, more specifically, the child, young person or adult needs to learn the skills that will give them the best chance of success. PBT encompasses all the skills needed and works well alongside existing strategies, programmes and policies.

All children crave attention and will be satisfied regardless of whether that attention is positive or negative. School systems and parenting skills experts promote rewarding positive behaviours. However, *any* type of attention can cause behaviours to be repeated.

'My dad has moved out and I hadn't seen him for ages. I was angry at him and shouted a lot at my mum. I was going to see him after school. I didn't know what to do. I was getting worried. My PBT mentor worked with me. We imagined all the

ways I could behave and what might happen. She reminded me that I could only choose for me, not my dad. I chose the two stories I liked best and we made a comic. I took it home and asked my mum what she thought. I decided the best way for me, and when I saw dad it worked OK.'
BETH, AGED 10

PBT opens the door to positive rewards and reactions that children are more in control of – this brings the side effects of happiness, contentment and pleasure, which in turn encourage repetition of better choices, which increases the likelihood of success. A definite win-win situation for all involved.

The majority of children who trialled PBT reported that they had noticed a change in their thinking.

'I used to think I was a "bad man" and I'd have to prove it all the time. I'd get involved in doing stuff like climbing on McDonalds' roof and spraying buses, and if anyone messaged me I'd go and fight them.

Now I'm not a "bad man" – I'm just normal – no higher or lower than anyone else. I feel free. Before I was stuck, I could only behave in the one way – bad. Now I can act how I really feel. I'm not in the gang now. I don't need them.

I'm doing more stuff like skateboarding and my mum lets me go out because she trusts me not to be in trouble all the time.'
HARRY, AGED 10

Becoming aware of how our thinking affects our behaviour can be a shock. So many times we react to real and imagined triggers without thinking – almost always only realizing the consequences of our actions once they have happened. PBT is a gentle technique or soft technology that uses a plastic card

or a soft neoprene band as a physical reminder to think before we act.

The consistent benefit reported by child users is that they feel better about themselves. They feel more in control of their behaviour, less anxious. They believe it is possible to act differently. Their responses include feeling 'normal'.

Children using PBT notice small changes straight away. Staff reports show a significant reduction in the number of behaviour incidents and a definite upward trend in the acquisition of school rewards for targeted pupils. Children react positively more often than not, and staff show greater awareness of situations that may need additional support or a session preparing the child for a situation or event.

Relationships between pupils and staff improve. Parents are able to maintain their support and are also reporting that changes extend into the wider aspects of the child's life. In some instances, the changes are so profound that staff reassess their opinions and start to believe that the changes will be permanent, which in turn changes their attitude towards the child – both conscious and unconscious. Studies have shown that up to 85 per cent of face-to-face communication is through body language.

The PBT keys to success are: Imagination, Choice and Action.

Imagination

When we look at a recipe book, a catalogue or a holiday brochure, it is our imagination and our memory that supplies us with the tastes, smells and sounds that make us want to taste the food, visit the place or buy the latest fashion.

If we teach children the skills they need to be self-responsible, think through choices and make reasoned decisions, we will all benefit.

'I didn't pay attention in class because I was always thinking about what had happened at playtime or what might happen at dinner time. I was always looking to see who was looking at me and thinking about fighting them. Now I can pause and think about what I'd like to happen instead. I'm learning more and concentrating better. I'm just enjoying my lessons and not being told off for not concentrating. I notice what I'm thinking now – I never used to. I was surprised when I found out how much I used to think about fighting. I feel happy at school now and I know people like me more.'
MICHAEL, AGED 10

Choice

What does the child want to change? This may not necessarily be what *you*/the adults in the child's life think they should change! How can you help them to explore what is possible? Our minds are magnificently complex – science has hardly begun to skim the surface of what is possible.

'My behaviour has been a problem to teachers ever since I was in the first year in school. I know when I'm doing wrong things, but I couldn't see any way to stop. When Mr D. asked if I'd like to do the PBT trial, I thought I'd say no, but I talked it through with my mentor and thought, "Why not?" I didn't think it would work because I thought, "I've been bad this long, how can that card change all my life?"'

I thought it sounded too easy – like if a remote control in my mind could change things. I'm going to secondary school this year and I don't want to be like this then.

So I started pressing Pause and imagining what I could do instead. The teachers helped me. It was hard. I had to keep remembering and my mentor reminded me too. My teacher put buttons on the wall and all the class practised pausing and thinking.

Before, I used to throw things and then calm down and think afterwards. I started to think Pause and then decide what to do if I felt upset. I had days between getting told off after just a few weeks, but I still didn't believe this would work for me – it felt like a dream where there was this good me and I thought I'd wake up and it would be back to how it was. I don't think that now.'

Giselle, aged 11

Seeing Yourself Differently

The mind does not distinguish in terms of time. When we re-live a positive memory, we can feel the feelings we felt at the time. This skill can be used to successfully create new neural pathways or habits just by visualizing or imagining ourselves in remembered or new situations.

> *The stories we tell ourselves become our story.*

Try This Simple Experiment

1. Relax and take a minute or two to remember a time when you were happy, confident, having fun, content – any positive emotion you like.

2. Imagine you are watching a film of yourself – see everything in as much detail as you can – make the film feel real.

3. Watch that other self in that situation.

4. How is s/he standing? Moving?

5. How is s/he talking? What is his/her tone of voice?

6. Make any changes or adjustments you want to.

7. Step into that remembered time and feel how it feels, see how it looks, hear how it sounds, tastes…

Action

Take the scenario out of your imagination and act on your choices. The easy way to do this is by repetition. Repetition creates habits; it reinforces the message and reminds us to act in certain ways. By practising regularly, this habit will be reinforced and you will be able to step into the future you have imagined. Acting in this way will help you to feel more of the feelings you like feeling more often.

> *'I hear and I forget. I see and I remember.*
> *I do and I understand.'*
> **CHINESE PROVERB**

How to Use PBT to Support Behaviour Change

Tips for Success

What follows is a brief explanation of the kinds of strategies that staff supporting children to use PBT have found most successful:

- When taking someone else (or yourself) through the PBT process, it is important to have high expectations of success and to challenge limiting beliefs. Believe that everyone has the resources they need and that solutions do lie within the individual.

- Before you start, create a safe, calm space where you are least likely to be disturbed or distracted. You may want softer lighting, comfy chairs or cushions.

- It helps to feel confident that this will work. Remind them of past achievements – i.e. 'You are good at...', 'Remember when...' – so they remember their own inner resources. Look for, and draw attention to, positives. Try using positive language to change negative statements.

- Believe this will work and convey it in your tone and body language. Use a friendly, enquiring tone. People take more notice of how we are and what we do than what we say – research shows that over 80 per cent of communication is non-verbal!

- The amount of time spent on the process will depend on circumstances. Remember, an advert can tell a story just as well as a film! This doesn't have to be a long process – 10 focused minutes are better than an hour for most children and teenagers.

- Match their mood – this can be exciting, engaging and fun. In fact, it works better when attention is fully engaged.

- Encourage them to talk/walk/draw/imagine their story. Kinaesthetic learners might like objects laid down to represent parts of their story; they may also describe it in terms of how they feel in their body. Visual learners like to imagine pictures or scenes. Auditory learners might like to tell the story and describe how they want the event to happen. Some people might use taste to describe feelings. It is important to encourage the person to build a story using their preferred style and then add in other aspects to make it more real.

It is important to ensure that users have opportunities to practise their new skill and become adept at it. Choices can be reinforced visually, kinaesthetically and aurally. How does it look, feel, sound?

Once they are completely happy, they press Play and their body, mind and memory will all act together to unfold the story, just how they believe it already exists. It has been proven that our actions arise from our beliefs – so change the belief and change the outcome.

Remember

This technique needs to be practised. The solution may need revisiting, reviewing and revising.

In shortened form, these are the four stages of the PBT process:

Pause	Identify the problem or issue. Think about, discuss, feel and imagine alternative ways to behave. Be creative about possible solutions and options. Ask the 'miracle' question: 'What would it be like if this worked?' Also ask: 'How will I know?', 'When will I know?' and 'What will it feel like?'
Think	Create alternative scenarios and try them out. Discuss or walk through the steps needed that will clarify the choice, or agree actions to best solve a problem. What are the consequences? The benefits?
Decide	Test using all the senses and feelings. Does it feel right? Rewind while making any changes. Create as many scenarios as needed to feel happy with your choice.
Act	Press Play again when you are satisfied – and then put the choice or decision into action. Remember, you can always Pause again and refine your chosen path. The choice is yours.

IN THIS CHAPTER YOU'VE LEARNED:

- Imagination, choice, action!
- Would you be able to wait for that second marshmallow?
- Visualizing consequences.

*Pause * Think * Decide * Act*

11

RIOTING, BULLYING: CHILDREN AND THEIR FEEDBACK

*'Destiny is not a matter of chance; it is a matter of choice.
It is not a thing to be waited for; it is a thing to
be achieved.'*
WILLIAM JENNINGS BRYAN

Apart from the Amazon rainforest and some deserts or icy wastes – there are probably remotes even in the remotest places! – let's assume that on all continents the idea of Pause, Play, Fast Forward and Rewind is well and truly part of the global language. Those five words are familiar to just about every child of – let's be conservative about this – six or older.

Soon you'll read about the experiences at schools trialling the use of PBT. More details come later in this chapter. For now, though, let's just think of those children who haven't yet had the PBT experience, and how they might benefit.

London and various other British cities suffered a summer like no other in 2011, with rioting and general mayhem spreading through the streets for no apparent reason.

Unfortunately, some of those involved were really quite young – 11 was the youngest quoted for the London area.[1] In the UK, the age of criminal responsibility is set at 10, so theoretically, these children/young teenagers could pay the price for not employing their own understanding of consequences.

More disturbing, looking from a parent's point of view, is the realization that some of the young people out on the streets must have been there with the unspoken 'agreement' of their parents. Not actually permission to go and loot, to be there to riot, but we'd ask if there were youngsters on the streets during those few days in the summer of 2011 whose mother or father simply didn't check where they were. Didn't stop and think… didn't press Pause and accept responsibility for their own children. It's a given that we all – parents up and down every street in every nation – make mistakes. But not knowing, not caring, not checking – not to put too fine a point on it, not *grounding* one's children at the first hint of trouble? What are the consequences?

Clearly, one of the outcomes is that they do something they shouldn't. That they know they shouldn't. That they perhaps haven't had the 'home training' (discipline?) to step away from. They haven't been brought up with a Pause Button of their own. Follow the chain of consequences through and you get to arrest, court, conviction, punishment, criminal record, struggles to find work in the future.

Yes, the rioters might have a pair of designer trainers in their wardrobe, but now they've maybe also got custodial sentences and criminal records. And what about the effects on their extended families – and society in general? How would the outcome have been different if they'd been taught to use PBT?

Two young girls, aged 13 and 14, who had been looting in one northern British city were told by a judge to pay £5 a week compensation from their pocket money. He held back from involving social workers because he felt that the distraught, sobbing parents (in this instance the couples involved were deemed hard-working, respectable people) were victims, too.[2]

He asked the girls to consider the consequences of their actions by looking across the courtroom and seeing the anguish and emotion of their mums and dads. *The girls were asked to see the consequences of their actions.*

Were the parents 'guilty' of not looking at consequences earlier in the disciplining of their girls? Nothing more than a speculative question, one worth spending a couple of minutes pondering.

Children need and like boundaries. With parents avoiding discipline for whatever reason, as yet unable to press Pause, they are not setting those boundaries. So the parent-child margin is more blurred, less clear-cut than it arguably needs to be.

Any parent conscious of TV favourites *Nanny 911* or *Supernanny* will actually already be well versed in the principles of PBT, though of course not by name. Consequences! Children misbehaving need to be warned that their behaviour will result in time out, the naughty step, whatever method you're using, so they can weigh up that choice for themselves and be prepared for the consequences of their actions. The principle of consequences in childcare is yet another virtuous circle: consequences lead to greater self-control, leads to self-discipline, leads to better consequences and so on…

If it's so glaringly obvious that a little person needs to recognize that their actions will have outcomes, shouldn't that apply to grown-up people just as much as the youngsters of the family?!

Bully-boy Tactics

Would a school bully see things differently if, during PBT training, he or she heard the story of those responsible for bullying one Yorkshire schoolboy?

This 13-year-old was hit with a wooden drawing board[3] after a teacher left the classroom to get assistance when a classroom bully became disruptive and verbally abusive. The boy needed hospital treatment after receiving arm and shoulder injuries. His mother became incensed when the school seemed likely to suspend the culprit for just two days, so she complained. He was subsequently removed from the school. In the first payment of its kind, the school made an undisclosed four-figure compensation payout to the boy's family after admitting a breach of statutory duty and negligence.

Might the bully have benefitted from PBT?

Might the teacher who left the room have benefitted from PBT?

Cyberspace Consequences

As any parent of pre-teens and teens can confirm, the growing-up previously done in the schoolyard, around the table in the school canteen, on the bus on the way home, and sometimes on the phone with our best mates, is now often being carried out on social networking sites.

No longer do youngsters practise their burgeoning vocabulary of expletives, tell (probably wildly exaggerated) tales of sexual exploits and generally grow up away from the public gaze. Not a bit of it. They're there seemingly every waking hour, surfing every available wave of online social interaction. Facebook, instant messaging, MSN, WhatsApp, Tweeting and using all manner of other 'virtual' communication devices!

Given that parents, too, know the potential of these sites as a way of 'checking up on' their children, mightn't everyone do well to press Pause whenever they're about to click 'Send'? OK, it's not really any different to the basic principle of not sending an email without double-checking what you've said and what impression it might give, but social networking sites are so... well... public. Not only do youngsters run the risk of upsetting, worrying or angering their parents, but there's more than a passing chance that some stranger might spot an ill-considered picture and target you (or your child). Which could lead to a torrent of unwanted emails, unpleasant picture messaging or, worse still, cyber-stalking or 'grooming'. A horrendous thought, and a message worth drumming into our sons and daughters at the earliest available opportunity.

About to paste a picture of yourself at the beach? Pause. Fast Forward to it being there, open for all to see, on the *World Wide Web* – that's its name, after all – and the kids at school taking the opportunity to make fun of you for your teensy bikini. Use your magnifying glass to see in glorious, embarrassing, shameful Technicolor the looks on your classmates' faces.

Hear the foul language, the merciless teasing you'll be subjected to. Rewind, Fast Forward to you having pasted a

totally different holiday pic – one with your mum and dad all fully clothed, having a lovely family time. Feel better? Happier about who might be looking and whether they'll be thinking of conning you online? Is that sufficient motivation to change your decision? Press Play and choose which picture to post.

About to put a message on your 'wall' about what happened with your two mates, a bottle of vodka and the spare room at a party? Press Pause. Fast Forward to once you've done it. You find out you made all sorts of incorrect assumptions. Both sets of parents are beside themselves with worry and have grounded the two friends who are now not best pleased with you. How do you feel about your message now?

Really stop and consider this. Don't just pay lip service to it – go there, feel it. See yourself. Take a deep breath; calm yourself to look, almost in slow motion, at how things will pan out. Do you think you will be feeling good about yourself, or rather immature and ridiculous? Rewind and Fast Forward again to a future in which you posted absolutely nothing. There was nothing concrete to tell people and, even if there was, you know it was no one's business but the couple involved. How do you feel now? Stop and really see yourself in that new situation, feel how you would feel. Happier, more comfortable with yourself, sure that your friends will know you're trustworthy? Once you're certain of your thoughts, make your decision as to which is the better course of action for you and press Play. A better present, right now!

One of your friends (maybe 'real', maybe 'virtual') is mouthing off in some rather unpleasant language about their family. You're a bit fed up that your folks won't allow you out as late as you want, and are pressuring you to revise for your upcoming exams. What wouldn't you give to just vent, there and then, online for everyone to see what boring, fuddy-duddy, harsh, awful people your mum and dad really are? Press Pause right now! Fast Forward to after you've let rip. Really given it some, with all barrels blazing. All the expletives, not deleted. Except you overlooked the fact that your mum is a Facebook friend so she sees everything you write. Now she's knocking on your bedroom door, not only angry that you would be so rude, but upset that you've used foul language, and disappointed with you in the way only mums can be. You're going to be in trouble for a little while after this one; you may lose the use of your laptop and you'll certainly have some work to do to be in her good books again.

So Rewind, Fast Forward and look at what will happen if you just bite your tongue and post to your friend that you're sorry you can't spend much longer chatting because you want to get good results so ought to be revising. You're thinking of your future, after all. Not just today, but tomorrow and where you want to be some way down the line. You might just tell your friend you know how she feels, but she'll probably feel better in the morning and, anyway, didn't her mum recently take her on a special girly outing, just the two of them? How much better would saying that make you feel? You will have been positive, encouraging, still friendly, much more mature and, what's more, if you do get some revision done your grades stand a good chance of being what you need to get to the university you're hoping for. A far better outcome all round. So make your choice of action, press Play and get on with life right now.

Never forget that the Internet is a tool used by many people for many different reasons. Many Human Resources departments actually request that an in-depth search be done on the names of people who've applied to be considered for vacancies. So if you're messaging all and sundry about your torrid summer affair, or blurting all the details of your alcohol-soaked weekend, it might not be only your friends reading it.

Of course, whenever you hear or see media debate about the influence of alcohol in modern society, at least part of the spotlight is on binge drinking by young people. Martin says they just don't see the long-term consequences of their abuse of alcohol. You can talk about the reduction of cost to the health system, which would be significant – running into millions – but what about the effect on young people's lives?

Putting the spotlight back on parents, how many can look deep into themselves and know they've not 'pushed' their child to sign up for a sport or activity simply because they think the child 'should', without considering the child's strengths, weaknesses and preferences? Or the reverse: a parent who doesn't want his son to have dancing lessons at school because he thinks it 'girly' – has this parent ever actually thought through the decision? Considered the boy's natural dancing ability?

Do 'hothousing' parents have to take responsibility for a Pause Button moment before taxiing their child here, there and everywhere, using up all the spare moments of the day, leaving no time for 'just being a kid'?

Do overweight or alcohol-dependent parents ever consider the example they're setting?

Do parents guilty of swearing in front of their children in the kind of vitriolic, racist language used by a south London woman on a tram in 2011,[4] realize the effect on their youngsters? (She had a toddler on her lap at the time of the incident, which went viral on the Internet.)

So many questions... but plenty of time to spend really thinking about your best choice, *if* you're using your Pause Button!

The Immaturity Issue

Today's young people have an added burden to contend with, which those born a few generations ago didn't. Young men are reaching their sexual peak earlier, leaving today's 18-year-old at the same level of physical maturity as the 22-year-old of 1800. But − and it's one of those big buts − a German researcher has now suggested that their brains haven't caught up, leaving them likely to continue taking the greater risks associated with youth.

Professor Joshua Goldstein, based in the German city of Rostock, was reported in 2011 to have used European records that identified a shift in the timing of young men's testosterone-triggered 'accident hump'. At a drop rate of 2.5 months every decade, their hormonal propensity for recklessness and accidents is now happening four years earlier than it was at the beginning of the 19th century. Since the shift happened before industrialization and the advent of cars (today we might tag these influences 'boys' toys'!), he explains it as a simple case of earlier maturity.

This clearly leaves a whole generation − and more − of young men in the 'snap-decision trap' addressed by PBT. As Professor Goldstein put it, earlier risk-taking among males could be dangerous because it occurs at an age when they are less mentally and socially mature.[5]

Insurance companies have been swift to leap on the bandwagon of recognizing this risk-taking age, offering a way to avoid the punitive car insurance premiums young men attract. A number of insurers now offer reduced premiums[6] to young and inexperienced drivers if they're prepared to install a 'black box' to track their driving performance and abilities.

And Now... Feedback (in Their Own Words)

Trial Results 2011

In the autumn term of 2011, six children with behavioural issues were selected from a large primary school in Birmingham, UK, and trained in how to use the PBT wristband/card to give them more thinking time before choosing how to act/react. The initial results make it clear that there were very swift, obvious and beneficial results.

Gay Jones, who has written Chapter 10 of this book, developed the system as trialled. Her enthusiasm for the PBT method is almost palpable.

She describes PBT as really catching her imagination, being deceptively simple and the missing link between NLP techniques, mindfulness and CBT. She says it's a tool that gets into the right bits of the brain.

She feels it has potential outside of mainstream education, too. In a trial with an eight-year-old boy high up on the autistic spectrum, he's found it really useful if he catches himself at the right time. If he goes into anger or a highly charged emotional state, it's too late. But if it's before that time, he's finding it quite effective. And for every time he does catch it, it's an improvement for him and everyone around him. And he's working together with his mum on it.

Across the Age Spectrum

PBT brings a new element in. With CBT and other therapies, it's essentially passive words, which could mean hours of talking. PBT takes this to a different level. If you have a reminder in your pocket or purse, or on your key ring, it's almost like a touchstone – physical proof that you're doing something different, changing something. It's a tool for self-responsibility and you're responsible for using it. The more you use it, the more responsible for yourself you become.

The key to it is hooking into the correct part of the brain. Hooking out of the thinking/doing part and hooking into the being part. The mindfulness, Buddhist practice part of it. When you are being, you aren't actually doing.

To use the 20:80 iceberg model, 20 per cent of the brain works in the conscious and 80 per cent in the unconscious. Of that 20 per cent conscious part, most of it is involved in thoughts: telling you what you must do, what you have to do, etc. Whereas if you can tap into the more powerful subconscious part, you can sometimes reverse that way of thinking. If you can do that, you can potentially reverse anything.

When someone's made you angry, and you're reactive, what comes to the fore is stress. You've gone back to the pre-Stone Age brain, or limbic brain, into fight-or-flight, survival mode. When you're like that, all your other systems shut down because the body's just concerned about saving you from whatever is threatening you. Then, because you're stuck in this reactive mode, you're not able to think clearly, not able to use any other part of your creativity or your problem-solving skills.

PBT clicks the restart button, and you have to learn to make it instinctual. Habitual.

For Gay this is exciting because it hooks into your thought processes. Makes the link between doing, being and action. She thinks it has potential because it's visual, because it's tactile, because it utilizes the preferred modality of the brain. It's about images and stories, about film, about creating pictures in the mind, as with some elements of NLP. It's above language. It goes deeper or beyond that, really.

Words – well you have to read, or understand language – but images? Well... almost everyone recognizes the symbols on a remote control!

Could It Possibly Be Too Simple?

Gay doubts it's possible for PBT to be too simple. She says it's simple on the surface – the 20 per cent on the surface. Underneath is the 80 per cent of how your brain works and where change is imprinted.

You don't have to know, with a remote control, that if you take it apart it's got a mother board, that it's got wireless works and the frequency is going to your TV at 186,000kph. You don't need to know all that's behind it – though if you're interested you can find out – for it to work.

Ultimately, with PBT, it's about using it often enough to create new pathways through the jungle of neural networks.

And the scope of uses for PBT? Gay is no less outspoken than Martin: 'Really, we could take it in any direction,' she says. 'And that makes it very exciting.'

As with many potential applications of PBT, expectations are realistic. Say a child's had his day of PBT with the teacher; he goes out into the playground, does something aggressive. Ends up in detention the next day. Then it's reinforced – what if you'd pressed Pause? What if you'd thought about the consequences?

People will maybe still do the 'wrong' thing, but if you can instil in them that they will then see the consequences of doing the 'wrong' or 'right' thing, it's just as valuable.

Gay is totally immersed in PBT and has thought through every aspect possible. Can she see downsides? 'The only thing I wondered was if it could be used to manipulate people – but of course the whole thing is dependent on their own thoughts, so definitely not. I can't see any downsides at all!'

So what did the parents, teachers and, possibly most important of all, the children involved in the school trials think of the PBT experience?

Daniel, 10, says, 'It's really helping me. I use it when people are annoying me and getting me angry. When someone's calling me names I just turn round and press the Pause button and it would just make me think of something else than the situation.'

So has he noticed a change in his behaviour? 'I think so,' he says. 'A couple of teachers have, too. It makes me feel like I can be good.'

Another 10-year-old, Jaden, expresses the change in himself quite succinctly. 'Before, I used to be nasty to people sometimes and now I'm a lot calmer.' He's gone from being in trouble every day to no problems at all within a half term. 'I wear the wristband all the time, at school and at home,' he explains. 'In the playground people start fights with me a lot so I press my Pause Button and that helps calm me down. It's the same thing every time: it makes me think "keep out of trouble."'

'My teachers say they've seen a big difference in my behaviour and I'm very happy. My mum says my behaviour is a lot better at home. Before, if I got mad at someone, I used to break stuff. Now I just press my band and go to my room and calm down. I'm happy.'

Two parents spoke about the results of the trial so far, as seen from the home viewpoint.

Georgie's 12-year-old daughter was prone to occasional temper tantrums and she was looking for alternative ways of helping her calm down and control her emotions. 'It's been a brilliant success – she obviously has her little outbursts at times, and I just say, "Use your bracelet," and she does. I don't always have to prompt her to use it; she tends to do it herself. It's had a really good effect.

'A couple of times she's used it at school – generally after arguments with her girlfriends and things like that. It can be upsetting and relatively traumatizing for a child when that happens, and they don't know how to express it, so she'll sit there and take a second. She's able to level her own emotions out.'

Georgie herself is also trying out the PBT wristband. '[My wristband] is always there; I can reach down and touch it. So it brings to the forefront of my mind that I can actually control... whatever – when I want to!'

Fern's eight-year-old son suffers from Autism and Attention Deficit Hyperactivity Disorder (ADHD). She describes him as having 'severe behavioural problems'. Only a few weeks after the PBT trial started, Fern was already reporting changes for the better.

'It's working really, really well,' she said. 'If I can compare the new school year with last year, he would have been put in the "calming down room" more or less every day for something he'd have flown off the handle for. It could be something quite tiny but he'd blow it out of proportion. This school year so far he hasn't been in once.

'There was an incident on the minibus where things got a bit taut between him and another child. Usually he'd have kicked off straight away, but he told me he felt his PBT band, thought about it and calmed himself down.

'I was really impressed. That's the first time I've heard about anything like that happening.

'Instead of flying off the handle he's been able to talk to his teachers about how he feels – why he doesn't want to do the work, how he's struggling with the work – rather than just grab a chair and throw it at somebody.

'He's a lot calmer for it. His teaching assistant has noticed a huge change in him, too. His teacher loves the idea and she says she thinks a lot of the other children in the school would benefit from the PBT band.'

What would she say to other parents? 'I'd say give it a go. What have you got to lose really? I've seen a real change in my son's behaviour, and he's got severe behavioural difficulties. If I can see the benefits for him it's the proof of the pudding that it does work.'

Here's a brief look at the responses of some other children who joined in the PBT trials:

Brett (10)

Brett hangs around with older boys and likes to be liked. He has been cautioned for setting fire to a waste bin and damaging property. He would like to stay out of trouble, but isn't sure how to resist the temptation to impress his older mates.

How Has PBT Helped You?

'It's helping me think more. Before, I'd have already been in the middle of something before I even thought – now I am choosing more. I still hang out with my mates, but I don't just do stuff because I'm told to all the time.'

Judith (8)

Judith is a quiet and nervous girl. When she is worried she bites her nails until they bleed. Her mum has painted them with chemicals, but she just can't stop biting them. She'd like to change this habit.

How Has PBT Helped You?

'I use it all day every day to remind me not to chew. Now I can press Pause before my fingers get to my mouth about three times out of every five. I think I can get better and stop biting my nails by Year 5.'

Colin (10)

Colin sometimes gets really angry and lashes out, shouting and throwing things. He knows that this is inappropriate, but can't seem to stop himself.

How Has PBT Helped You?

'I use it at home and at school and at after-school clubs. I use it most for stopping fighting. The band works. I got rewards from the teacher. I might get Star of the Week – that's the best award in school – I feel happy.'

Anil (11)

Anil has little space at home and often physically hurts other children if they knock into her. She often misses breaks and doesn't seem to be able to understand boundaries and rules.

How Has PBT Helped You?

'Before, physical stuff would make me aggressive, now I like dinner time better because I'm calmer. I like not being in trouble all the time and I do more work in class.'

Jak (9)

Jak daydreams instead of doing his classwork. He is often tired and spends time at home watching videos and playing on his Xbox. He will be moving into Year 6 and wants to do well in his SATs, but can't seem to stop drifting off instead of concentrating.

How Has PBT Helped You?

'I like that the PBT sessions are about making up stuff. I'm good at that and I make good stories. I'm doing better at starting and stopping and finished my work in class time three times last week. It [the PBT card] is like a reminder to stop, think and do my work.'

Darren (11)

Darren has a statement of special educational needs (SEN) for his ADHD. He finds it hard if too many things are asked of him at once. He says his head just 'starts whirling around' and he can't think.

How Has PBT Helped You?

'Sometimes I imagine a big button on the floor – it freezes my brain and blanks my head. It takes my mind off it. My mum has noticed a difference – I think the school rang her to say. I'm pleased about that.'

Julia (10)

Julia loves sweets and crisps. She refuses to eat any 'proper' meals other than at school. She is overweight for her age and feels unhappy, so she eats more sweets. She says she hates her size and wants to be 'normal'.

How Has PBT Helped You?

'I use the band to help me choose healthy food more often now. My mentor has done me a chart and I give myself a star every time I make a healthy choice and I've got 37 stars already. I like the way pressing Pause makes me remember to think before I eat. I like the PBT sessions. They make me feel special and I'm proud I can think of other things to do.'

School Deputy Head Jim Thomson and Pastoral Manager Nigel Rivers both report noticeably calming results within very few weeks of starting the PBT trials. Nigel takes up the story: 'I look after the welfare and behaviour in school, ranging from vulnerable children and child protection issues, to behaviour. So when the kids are displaying a lot of negative behaviour I have to deal with them.

'The reason we did PBT initially was to target certain children that aren't responding positively when being told off, or when there's a punishment or consequence they weren't responding very well to. We chose six and gave them a wristband and the remote control card to wear around their neck, just to see whether they could take it on board and think before they act.

'We would have a weekly session on a Monday, when we prepared them for the week of PBT, and what that would include was one-to-one work with myself and the child to remind them how they could best use PBT; and then on a Friday to see if any scenarios have happened throughout the week. If they've had to use it, and if they could have used it differently.

'PBT has helped the school tackle behaviour in a different way. We've used it quite positively in tackling the six children — where they were displaying a lot of anger and a lot of negative attitudes towards other children and peers in the playground, we've seen a dramatic change in how they would use it. What I'm noticing is that they're thinking a lot more before displaying the anger. That's not to say it's a quick fix, not to say it's working 100 per cent of the time, but it's preventing them most of the time from getting into trouble. It's working really well.'

The parents, too, have become involved in the trial. 'We gave the bands to the parents so they could experience it as well; what it was like to think before they act,' said Nigel. 'We've noticed that instead of shouting and yelling, they'd have to think what was the best way to deal with the child at home — a lot of parents were saying they'd think, "Well, he's expressing an emotion or behaviour, let me think about it and see what's the best way to deal with them."'

'Parents have been saying they've been using it together with the child, who's been talking to them about their own actions and expressing their own feelings and thinking about how best to act before a scenario. The parents have noticed a dramatic change. I think also it's building their relationship with their children, which is a really good thing and a positive way forward for the family.'

And in the future? Nigel sees the prospect of rolling the trial out to more children – those who are withdrawn, not expressing themselves as much as staff would like them to, or those who've become isolated or withdrawn emotionally. 'Hopefully for the future with the other children we use, we'll notice a change in them as well,' he says.

Deputy Head Jim Thomson is used to complex and challenging behaviour of the kind encountered on many city estates. He identifies two major problems in finding ways of engaging the children about their behaviour, and how best to involve parents in tackling this kind of problem.

'We're finding that some of the traditional ways of dealing with challenging behaviour are really taxing for the teachers. Maybe we should be updating our way of thinking because there's a lot of talk about strategies for behaviour, but they tend to be complex and new teachers need to find something that is easy, manageable – and manageable to the extent that they're not spending hours and hours wading through books and paperwork.

'They have other issues in school to deal with, and we're finding that PBT seems to be the easy way of dealing with challenging behaviour, which the children understand, the staff understand and, what's more, probably for the first time, the parents understand.

'Over the years I think we forgot to involve parents in strategies for dealing with challenging behaviour. With PBT we can engage with all three parties – school, parents and children – and work together to enable progress to be made across all spectrums of challenging behaviour.

'Parents are crying out for a simple way of dealing with issues at home, and working together we think we'll be highly successful with something that is so easy to administer but so complex when you start looking at it deeply. The children we've piloted this with have found it useful.

'They are happy to be involved with this. It's up to date. It's very much now. I think because of this, the children want to succeed and are making great inroads into helping us help them and their parents dealing with issues.'

A PAUSE BUTTON MOMENT

Father of three Barry's bad temper meant almost anything could make him 'flip'; sometimes he would be aggressive and verbally abusive. His wife and children feared for their lives when, one minute he would be normal and the next a raging ball of anger.

Barry was introduced to PBT by an anger management counsellor, and liked the idea of stopping to think, imagining the consequences and making a choice as an alternative to flying off the handle as he had been.

It wasn't long before Barry felt the anger build up inside of him. The children were being particularly loud and his first instinct was to shout, but he remembered to press Pause and think for a moment about his actions and the consequences. On Rewind, he could see another scenario with the more positive outcome he would prefer. Once ready to choose his action, he pressed Play and turned to the children. 'Stop being so loud! Don't forget tomorrow is pocket money day and there's none for loud monsters,' he joked, and everyone was quiet – and happy.

IN THIS CHAPTER YOU'VE LEARNED:

- Children need boundaries; to have boundaries it helps to have outcomes.
- School success stories.
- Visualizing consequences.

*Pause * Think * Decide * Act*

12

PUTTING YOUR 'SENSIBLE HEAD' ON

'Life is a sum of all your choices.'
ALBERT CAMUS, FRENCH AUTHOR,
PHILOSOPHER AND JOURNALIST

Elsewhere in the book we've talked about inbuilt behavioural issues – we've also covered ill-judged snap decisions, and how allowing triggers to kick in plays a part in making poor choices.

Later in this chapter we'll look at the poor choices made by some well-known people which have led to them appearing, sometimes daily, in the pages of tabloid newspapers worldwide. Of course, you might conclude that they've got the money, and often the power, to help them 'ride out' their mistakes.

More important to *your* life though, than these well-chronicled errors of judgement, are your own. Essentially, we're all fallible. There's a good firm case for suggesting that you can actually put PBT into use in many other normal day-to-day scenarios, giving you, your friends and colleagues, and every Joe and Jane Bloggs out there the benefit of a 'second chance' to re-think what they're doing.

We're not talking necessarily about deep-seated and repetitive errors, but those occasions when they (you) really should have known better, should have – or, at the very least, *could* have – spent just a few moments considering what to do to get a less dramatic outcome. Made a better choice for you and those around you. As with all PBT moments, it just requires a moment of frozen time, a second or two in the Pause Button safe mode.

Of course, the more thorough consideration you give a situation, the better the likely outcome. Stopping and considering is a good start, but taking it a step further to actually 'seeing' the possible consequences – like a film played out in front of you – that's the challenge. And as we've said, this is equally applicable in everyday situations and in tackling problem behaviours.

Talking scarecrow Worzel Gummidge, beloved character of Barbara Euphan Todd's books and the British TV series, had various interchangeable heads[1], sometimes giving him a particular skill which he could choose at will. Maybe you could look at your options that way, too… to help you spot those moments when you really should select your 'sensible head'.

For example, you're doing some home improvements, decorating a hallway or a high outside wall. You're using your ladder. But your toddler was poorly last night and you were up for hours. Now you're exhausted, even though it's only just after lunch. Are you thinking clearly? Have you truly thought out whether the ladder's placed correctly? It will only take you a moment to press Pause. If you don't check the base of the ladder, and it slips, what will the consequences be? Injury for you? Distress for your family? Maybe even loss of earnings, which impacts on everyone around you?

How would you feel if that very toddler was walking – unsupervised, raising another set of questions about your judgement – past the ladder when it slipped, and it wasn't just you who was injured? The choices and consequences mount up at every turn when you start really thinking things through.

Impulse: a sudden wish or urge that prompts an unpremeditated act or feeling; an abrupt inclination.[2]

Or say you're at work, it's going home time and a very attractive co-worker suggests you pop to the bar for a 'quick one' on the way home – to give you a chance to 'brain dump' a particular problem in that project you're collaborating on. Should you press Pause and think through the possible ramifications? Neither of you has any plans to 'hit' on the other, and indeed you don't, but maybe the following day your colleagues at work put two and two together and make five, and start the rumour mill running… which then has knock-on consequences for you, for them and for both of your careers/families. Will your boss compliment the pair of you for the insight achieved in that chat you had, or will they think there's no smoke without fire and never quite trust either of you to work together again? Or you go, have one too many and actually *do* allow passions to become inflamed, with all the attendant professional- and (potentially) relationship-wrecking consequences.

You're fond of the open air, and on the way back from a work appointment in a distant country town, decide on a whim to go for a long walk on a big hill some way from home. What you fail to do, though, is Pause, thinking ahead about weather, unfamiliar countryside, etc. You just don't stop, take a deep breath and really consider what might happen. You leave your car where no one else knows you'll be, your mobile has very little battery left, you don't have a very good map (if any map at all), you're wearing light clothing and have only a cardigan with you – and realize about a mile from the car that you had sweets and water in the car but have forgotten them. So… do you head off up the hill anyway? Or press Pause, think you should have known better and go back to the car for the water and sweets? Press Pause and visualize all the possible hazards of setting off into unknown territory ill-prepared, and decide you can always take that walk another day?

Your kitchen badly needs more plug space, but rather than wait to book an electrician, you decide you've helped friends before, you know a bit, it's not that complicated to put a new socket in. You'll do it yourself. Pause. Please. Will you Pause? Or might you plough on without checking out the depth of your knowledge? What would the consequences be if you didn't involve a more knowledgeable friend, or do plenty of research first? Would you leave some cable just a tiny bit loose, which, over time, would leave the socket dangerous? Sure, you might press Pause and know that, yes, your confidence is justified. But without that Pause, just think what could happen sometime down the line. And who might it happen to? You? Your baby son crawling around at socket height? What would happen? Would he get a powerful electrical shock, stop breathing, only to be found lifeless by your distraught wife or elder daughter? Would that be one of the consequences you ought to have considered?

Winter time. You need to drive to the other end of the county, but it's just started snowing. Off you go… do you remember all the warnings and reminders you've ever heard about taking a blanket, spade, flask of hot drink; making sure you have your mobile with you? What consequences might occur if you didn't?

Would pressing Pause give you that thinking time so you don't rush off ill-prepared? It's so simple when you see it written down, isn't it?!

Another journey – only half a mile down to a friend's house for your children to spend the morning while you plan some school event. No need to put seat belts on. At least you think so, because you haven't *really* thought it through. A Pause moment, a Freeze Frame, would give you the chance to see how really short-sighted your decision would prove if that wayward local teenager just happened to be out on his over-powered motorbike and came ploughing across the junction. Of course, you may have time to slam on your brakes. But without her seatbelt, your little one would have nothing to stop her shooting between the front seats and being badly injured on the dashboard. Freeze frame as she lunges towards a fractured collarbone or life-changing facial scarring. So easy. Pause. Think of the consequences. Think of the alternative consequences. Rewind. Make a decision. Play.

'Safety doesn't happen by accident.'
Anonymous

There's a school of thought that suggests PBT was previously not necessary, for various reasons. The extended families of the past would see senior relatives handing down generations' worth of advice; passing on homilies and clichés about not leaping out of the frying pan into the fire, making sure you eat an apple a day, better safe than sorry and so on – not only making life safer, easier and less stressful, but demonstrating some of the core principles of PBT!

Latterly, the so-called 'nanny state' took on the mantle that was beginning to be cast off with the rise in the numbers of women going out to work, and introduced campaigns to teach children how to ride bikes safely, how to cross the road, even dealing with how all of us should cope in the event of a nuclear blast! More recently this has developed (arguably, over-developed) into a minefield of political correctness that leaves few risks available even to be experienced. Witness counties in the UK where horse chestnut trees have signs put on them to warn of the danger of falling conkers.[3] Where plant troughs are not allowed to be put on balconies. Where children are not allowed to compete in minor sporting events in case of injury. Where first aiders are not prepared to help the injured for fear of a law suit. Where rubbish collection staff are not allowed to cross a road just 20 feet wide to empty bins, in case they're knocked down en route.[4]

Without experiencing risks, though, how can anyone learn the fundamentals of recognizing and judging the potential consequences and accompanying responsibilities of their actions?

Grandmothers and grandfathers of generations past would effectively have been teaching youngsters their own Pause Button control system… think first, act later. Look before you leap. A stitch in time saves nine. Act in haste, repent at leisure. You get the picture!

> 'Hug your kids at home, but belt them in the car.'
> **ANONYMOUS**

No one's perfect; every one of us makes at least one choice, decision, judgement every day that we might regret. In all probability, several. Why? If people we know are anything to judge by – and they're not unusual, not special – it's because there's a constant rush about life these days. Do we fail to give ourselves thinking time because we're in such a terrible hurry?

We *think* we're in such a rush? We can't imagine there's a single second to stop and reflect before doing anything? Really? How illogical is that?!

You're on your way to answer the phone and you overlook the fact that when the phone rang you were in the kitchen making supper and your three-year-old is still in there, intrigued by the bubbling pot over there on the stove. Can the person on the other end of the phone not wait another 15 seconds while you turn the cooker off and move the pan out of reach? Even if they *do* ring off, which was more important, answering the call or making sure your child is out of harm's way? You can easily find the number and ring them back. Was the rush really justified?

That same phone can be heard ringing just as you're soaping your younger child in the bath. Your head is saying, 'Answer the phone, get that phone, must get that phone.'

But your head will end up all over the place if you do that, find it was a cold-caller or, worse still, one of those 'silent' computer-generated sales calls, or your friend wanting to unburden herself and you know you should listen but there's a better time, later, when... and then realize the bathroom is silent. No splashing sounds. Were those 15 seconds grabbing a towel to take your snuggly clean baby to the hall with you really too much to ask? Why not Pause just for a second to think? Really think if answering that phone call is worth it? Worth, not to put too fine a point on it, the life of your child?

Thinking through the consequences of your actions is such a simple, obvious, basic concept, yet one we disregard so readily. Without thinking of the consequences!

> *'Chance-takers are accident-makers.'*
> **ANONYMOUS**

Just how many decisions do you make every day? 10? 20? 200? It could easily be 500 or 1,000, if you consider the number of things you do in any given 24-hour period. You've very probably had to think for a moment before many of them. Or perhaps you should have. Not all will have needed much contemplation, but maybe your life would be easier and less stressful if you *had* taken that bit longer?

It would be so easy, maybe even lazy, to suggest you need to be pressing Pause at every single moment of choice in your life. That would take up far too much time, time you'd be better using just living! But – and it's a but with a capital B and no mistake – we would suggest that it'll be a valuable use of some of that time if you (a) read this chapter, (b) recognize times when situations we've described ring true in your own life, (c) analyze how you could have thought a bit longer about possible consequences and (d) learn and re-learn that Pause Button process until it's as much a part of your routine as brushing your teeth and saying please and thank you. Then you will have the mechanisms and tools in place to help you identify those split-second decisions needing a Pause sequence, *before* you've made the wrong choice, wrong decision, wrong judgement, with all the consequences that could follow.

> *'Precaution is better than cure.'*
> **EDWARD COKE**

Everyday stuff. Everyday errors. Pause Button Therapy could help change all that.

One potential everyday occurrence sent to tax us is the role of the traffic warden (or whatever name these officials go by in your part of the world). Not for Martin the 'red mist' if he gets a ticket. He says how we react to traffic wardens is bad: they're trained, but maybe *we* should be trained to stop and think. Why should we get angry just because they've done their job correctly? They see our car parked illegally and approach us – and we're fit to explode. Do we ever stop and think what it's like to be in their shoes? We could approach the situation angrily, but what good is that going to do?

Press Pause. What will be the consequences of losing your temper, being rude and all that you know very well goes with it? Will you get a fine you mightn't have got because actually, they were feeling lenient and were just going to give you a warning? Will you bang your fist on your car in a temper and dent it? Will you put your blood pressure through the roof? What if, instead, you Rewind, Fast Forward and see the alternative: behaving calmly, apologizing for your stupidity, saying you accept they've got their job to do? Do you think there's a chance they might just tear up the ticket because it's so rare to be treated civilly? OK, maybe not likely, but at the very least you'll go home calm rather than wound up. Rewind, and make your decision.

Still with transport, what if you were one of those bus drivers who has absent-mindedly driven under a low bridge, endangering – and sometimes ending – the lives of those on the upper deck of his vehicle? Is absent-mindedness just another way of describing 'short-sightedness' or 'mindlessness', as opposed to 'mindfulness'? If drivers of any vehicle employed the technique of keeping a mental running commentary as they went on their route, might those people affected by incidents like the low bridge have benefitted from Pause Button moments by another name?

Driving a vehicle is a day-to-day occupation for many people, and one that can have serious repercussions for others. Consequences. 'Driver Falls Asleep at the Wheel'... How many times have you read that headline? And how many lives have been lost as a result? You're dozy because of the hypnotic effects of oncoming headlights? Pause. Literally find somewhere to stop. Consider the consequences of continuing your journey. That Pause may need to be 10 minutes of shut-eye, but you really do need to think through the result of plodding on, gradually getting drowsier and drowsier, and eventually smashing into whatever, whoever. Imagine the consequences. See the news report in your mind's eye. Then Rewind, make a decision and choose what is the mindful thing to do.

It's hard to conceive until you think about it, but maybe there's a use for PBT for families going through a hard time. Maybe someone's ill – even terminally ill. There are several ways to react to this, as there are always many more ways than one to react to just about everything. You can be sad, angry or anxious, and your mood could dull the ill person's mood and make their last weeks even more depressing. Or you could be positive, happy, live your life and help them live their life, to the fullest. Celebrate with them the time you have left together.

Which will help them most? Don't we sometimes have to hold back on feelings, even if it's not what we particularly want to do? Is it what's best for the person who's ill, and for family and friends? Does it help the situation or hinder it? Sometimes it will, sometimes it won't. You have to make a judgement call, don't you? Isn't that just as much a Pause Button moment as all the others we've suggested?

Are you in a relationship? Many of us are. Prepared to sacrifice it for a 10-minute 'quickie'? Many people are. Pressing

Pause might be the better bet. You're happily married, good job, car, young son, little daughter, everything's fine, weekend course away, leggy Sally's there and offering it on a plate...

What would the full consequences of this brief sexual encounter be? Do you see the value of looking thoroughly at all the consequences?

Maybe, given how much children pick up from observing their parents, we should be using PBT quite early on in the life of a family. What about the couple in relationship therapy? The husband's blaming the wife, the wife blaming the husband, and this is all going on in front of the children as well (if they're honest). What if they both just sat back, took a breath, pressed Pause and thought about the part each of them is playing. How they're individually responsible for changing the dynamics of their relationship. If they stayed in the PBT zone for long enough to see there are always at least two ways of going forward; if only one of them were to say to themselves, 'What if I tried it this way for a week?' Fast Forward and think how they would feel, how the relationship would feel, a week from now if they'd made some changes and the relationship had taken on a different dynamic. Would their husband/wife be happier? Would the friction have been reduced? Would the children be more settled? Rewind, Fast Forward to doing nothing. What would change? Nothing... except maybe for the worse. So? Rewind again, consider both outcomes, and make your choice. Play.

What about someone working in an office situation and having a good relationship with someone of the opposite sex – sharing cakes, going for a coffee or a drink after work – all innocent and amicable; then it gets to the stage of maybe going to the next level. Same as the previous example, just maybe a little more long-winded, a little more complex. A little more thought required beforehand. Do we only see the pleasure at hand? What about the after-effects on the marriage, the children. What about breaking our parents' hearts? Maybe driving a wedge between them and their grandchildren. Only spending one Christmas with one parent, one with the other. The ramifications for the extended family are enormous. All for a relatively meaningless sexual encounter. Is it really worth it?

A few moments spent in the safe zone of PBT could give you ample opportunity to see all these bad consequences – and see the good alternatives – and come out at the end ready to make a mindful decision. Mindful rather than knee-jerk. Or lustful. It just takes a bit of thought.

In all honesty, no one is likely to completely stop making mistakes. You're never going to get perfection. All you want is to get closer to it. You want to win the battles that matter and let the other ones roll.

Let's look at 21st-century communications. Who doesn't have a mobile and send a text daily, possibly hourly? And, as we've said earlier, with texting and instant messaging, tablets, notebooks, smartphones, Twitter, MSN, Facebook, etc., etc., all of those come with a whole lot more chances to foul up by not pressing Pause.

We no longer get the time to write a letter and check it over before sending it. It's a recipe for war and it ruins relationships. People lose their jobs through instant messaging. Just Pause first! Type it in if you like, but before you press Send, just stop. Take two minutes, go for a stroll, walk round the block, go to the toilet – whatever you want to do – *then* decide whether the tone and the way the message you've created looks makes it safe to be sent. Then, and only *then*, press Send.

How many of us have sent a text or an email only to wish the next day (or even the next instant) that we hadn't? We know everyone reading this will say, 'Yes, I have.' We've all done it. Martin says he's got in so much trouble from texting, with repercussions still reverberating today. He says he should never have sent the text, never should have worded it the way he did. But he never thought about the consequences. And he swears he's not going to let that happen again! Now any email he writes goes to draft first, to avoid over-reacting if there's a lot going on at the time.

Have you ever considered what we mentioned in Chapter 4 – some theories of Professor Philip Zimbardo about past, present and future thinkers? He makes a point in his writing about people who floss. People who floss their teeth, he maintains, are future thinkers.[5] They're thinking about the future of their teeth, of their mouth and of their health generally. He talks about good students being future thinkers. Some, told to do some work for three months' time, will go off and party. Others do it straight away.

They have the thought process: 'Let me stop and think about this: I can either use a bit of time each night and not go out for the whole of the weekend every week, and get it done in time.' They're future thinkers. They've thought about the consequences, not only of handing the work in late, but also of maybe getting a poor degree, or even no degree. Maybe less income, poorer housing choices, etc.

It's just a question of spending that bit of extra time in Pause mode.

If you're in work, it's an unfortunate fact of modern life that you're one of the 'lucky' ones. If you're actively looking for work, one thing you really should do is press Pause when you're preparing your CV or resume.

Unlike the creators of the following, who really should have checked (and double-checked!) to make sure their offerings were going to do them justice:[6]

'Career break in 1999 to renovate my horse'

'Skills: Strong Worth Ethic, Attention to Detail, Team Player, Self-motivated, Attention to Detail'

'I am great with the pubic'

Hobbies: 'Having a good time'

'Seeking a party-time position with potential for advancement'

What do you suppose were the consequences when their would-be employers received these? How long would it have taken just to press Pause before posting off these applications, or sending them by email? Pause and, having taken a deep breath, read, re-read and read again to ensure no errors put paid to your employment prospects.

This may sound flippant, but any one of those applicants may have been relying on getting that post to pay for a relative's medical bills, or a new car to ferry the children to school, or pay the family's way out of debt. The choice was of course theirs, and they chose to be short-sighted and mindless, rather than mindful, about how to proceed.

If 'ill-judged' is a description of the decisions made without recourse to pressing Pause, let's just take a sideways look at the definition of ill-judged. That definition is: short sighted. The definition uses a visual analogy. You've not looked well enough at what you need to think about; not looked far enough ahead to make a considered choice.

You should have used your Pause-Fast Forward... should have used your PBT remote!

Front-page Fallibility

At the time we started to put the ideas for this book together, we had no doubt at all that if anyone picked up any tabloid newspaper or 'popular' magazine – certainly in the UK but probably in most other countries as well – and turned to a page at random, there would be a good chance that at least one story would contain a person, or a scenario, that would benefit from PBT.

How many of those stories might never have made it to the newsstands if the people involved had practised PBT?

- French film star Gerard Depardieu was removed from a plane in Paris after causing a scene and urinating into a bottle while seemingly drunk.

- The wife of the Speaker of the British Parliament, Sally Berkow, did a slightly risqué magazine photo shoot early in 2011 wearing nothing but a strategically draped sheet. Within a couple of months she was also taking part in the reality TV show *Celebrity Big Brother*.

- Former US President Bill Clinton had a well-publicized dalliance with White House intern Monica Lewinsky.

- British businessman Gerald Ratner crippled his own jewellery business with one joke during a 1991 speech. Making such a gaffe is now known universally as 'doing a Ratner'. Referring to the cheap price of some decanters, he said, 'People say how can you sell this for such a low price? I say because it's total crap.' Shortly after that speech, his business was worth £500 million less than it had been.

- Suave British actor Hugh Grant was arrested for lewd conduct after an 'incident' in a car in Los Angeles with prostitute Divine Brown.

- Pop princess Britney Spears married childhood pal Jason Alexander in the early hours of the morning of January 3, 2004 in Las Vegas. Within 12 hours she'd filed for annulment; 55 hours later they were no longer husband and wife.

- Michael Jackson caused a stir when he dangled one of his children, head covered, from a third-floor hotel balcony.

- Golfer Tiger Woods, 'outed' as a serial cheater, finally publicly admitted, 'I was unfaithful. I cheated. What I did was not acceptable, and I'm the only person to blame.'

- New York Governor Eliot Spitzer resigned in 2008 after being discovered as a regular patron of prostitutes.

- Former UK Home Secretary David Blunkett faced publicity about an affair with a mainstream political magazine editor.

- Then-UK Health Minister Edwina Currie resigned after making an inaccurate claim that most of British egg production was at the time infected with salmonella.

- Within an hour of the 9/11 attacks, UK Labour spin doctor Jo Moore emailed her department's press office suggesting it would be a good day to release 'bad news' (at the time councillors' expenses had been making headlines). From this incident grew the phrase 'a good day to bury bad news'.

- Dior designer John Galliano was sacked for making anti-Semitic remarks while in a bar in Paris.

- Former football player turned UK TV pundit Andy Gray was sacked, and co-presenter Richard Keys resigned, after they made on-air sexist comments about a woman referee.

- British actor Jude Law had an affair with his children's nanny; he was quoted as saying, 'There is no defence for my actions, which I sincerely regret.'

- Pop superstars Rihanna and Chris Brown were all over the headlines when a text received on Brown's phone from another woman, and seen by his then-girlfriend Rihanna, sparked a row. Brown ended up accused of assaulting Rihanna, who, according to varying reports, had received eye, forehead and hand injuries.

> *'Was the pregnancy planned or just irresponsibility?'*
> **UK TALK SHOW HOST JEREMY KYLE TO GUEST, 23.05.11**

Chances are you are getting the picture now. Being a celebrity doesn't give you a Get Out of Jail Free card. In fact, there are those in the industry who feel that the very nature of people who become famous makes them doubly disposed to 'put their foot in their mouths'.

US university professor Roberto Weber of Carnegie Mellon University is an expert in the psychology of decision-making. He sums it up like this: *'The reason these people are celebrities is because they're not good at self-regulating.'* He feels celebrities live surrounded by the feeling of being rewarded for outrageous behaviour and attention-seeking. They can't gauge when what they are doing is inappropriate.[7]

Famous or infamous, A, C or Z-list, world champion or has-been, celebrities are no different to anyone else when it comes to decision-making. There is a tendency to see them as somehow special, occasionally untouchable, by the rules, regulations, morals and ethics that apply to the rest of us. They may have a stable of flunkies and hangers-on they can blame when things go wrong, but ultimately the buck stops with them.

Time to get a newspaper and add in your own Pause Button Moment suggestions!

> *'Speak when you're angry, and you'll make the best speech you'll ever regret.'*
> **LAWRENCE J. PETER**

A PAUSE BUTTON MOMENT

As Paul swung his legs over the side of the bed a few moments after the alarm went off, he felt that inevitable cough coming on. It was almost as regular as the clock. He knew why, of course. It was the cigarettes. Those things he felt he couldn't live without. Those things he yearned for after a meal, reached for as he took a sip of coffee, craved as soon as he knew a stressful phone call was coming.

Once he'd heard of PBT, he thought there was at least another chance to ditch the fags. After all, he'd tried that many times already. With PBT, though, when he pressed Pause it gave him the 'safe zone' in which he could think through all the smell, the cough, the cost, the aggravation, how he couldn't smoke in public places – all the many downsides. He could see his own red face as he almost choked every morning; he could feel the despondency at his own inability to take control. He even had time to think through how illogical most of his so-called 'reasons' for smoking were. Did nicotine help his stress? No, it raised his blood pressure. Having pressed Rewind and Fast Forward again he could see how he would feel if he managed a day, a week, maybe a month without giving in to the cigarette habit. He would start ditching the tar from his lungs within such a short time. How good would that feel? How much more in control would he be? Still within the PBT zone, he could then make his decision and press Play and get on with a less smoky, more healthy life.

The Self-service Checkout

You bought this book for a reason — to address specific behaviours, problems and consequences that have been affecting your life.

We've set out to explain how PBT came about, how truly simple it is to understand, yet also how it is based on clear psychological foundations. You've been encouraged to be brutally honest with yourself as to just what changes would make your life better. We've talked you through how, when and why you could be pressing Pause. We've shown how important it is to understand — *really* understand — consequences, and how extraordinarily wide-ranging they can be.

We've talked of creating new habits, and how to nip your own thought processes in the bud. We've looked, several times, at all the consequences of your actions when you use your 'virtual' remote. We've seen how easily children learn — and benefit from — PBT. We've taken a relatively light-hearted look at some celebrity meltdowns and how they could have been averted.

In the Appendix to this book, Theano Kalavana describes the science behind PBT's success. Ultimately, though, it's down to you and your 'Sensible Head'. You can — and should — refer back to the different chapters of this book whenever you feel the need. But you can go away positive, knowing that with just the simple process of pressing Pause you can halt the patterns that have played havoc with your life (or that of your friends, family members, etc.) for so long.

We're here to help, both in the book and on the website (www. pausebuttontherapy.com), but for you the real work begins now. We have pointed you in the right direction, now it's over to you.

Remember:

1. Identify the moment – that nanosecond when you need to think 'stop'. This is the hardest part. It's learning which situations you need to stop and think about, and which you don't.

2. Press Pause. Now you're safe, you have a breathing space, thinking time; just as long as you want…

3. Now Fast Forward to see, smell, and feel the results of what you're about to do. This allows you to experience in detail the fallout of what you are thinking of doing or saying.

4. Rewind, then Fast Forward to the second option. Repeat the visualization and feel the positive feelings, the sense of control.

5. Rewind again and decide which of these actions you are going to take.

6. Press Play and get on with your life.

IN THIS CHAPTER, YOU'VE LEARNED:

- How many decisions do you make every day?
- Do you put your sensible head on every time?
- Visualizing consequences.

---

*Pause * Think * Decide * Act*

TELL US YOUR STORIES!

As you know probably too well, not using a Pause Button can play havoc with anyone's life. From ill-judged texts and raised blood pressure to lost clients, the possibilities are, as they say, endless.

What's your worst story? Visit www.pausebuttontherapy.com and go to the Real Stories page, where you can key in your tales of woe. We'll send a PBT wristband and PBT remote device to the best received each month, as well as publishing them on the website.

Appendix

FUTURE-THINKING AND PBT: AN ACADEMIC PERSPECTIVE – Dr Theano V. Kalavana, PhD Health Psychology

*D*r Theano V. Kalavana received her PhD in the area of Health Psychology in 2007 from the University of Cyprus. She completed her Bachelor of Science in Philosophy, Education and Psychology, with Specialization in Psychology, at the National and Capodistrian University of Athens, Greece, and she received her Master of Science in Health Psychology from the University of Surrey, UK.

Her main area of research focuses on the contribution of self-regulation cognitions and skills in altering health behaviours. In 2007, as a Fulbright Scholar, she travelled to the US (Carnegie Mellon University, Pittsburgh; Pittsburgh Mind Body Center [PMBC]; and the Wellness Institute, Memorial Hospital of Northwestern University, Chicago) for her further training on self-regulation and health. In the past few years she has been teaching as Visiting Lecturer in the Department of Psychology at the University of Cyprus, and at the Department of Nursing, Faculty *of Health of the Cyprus University of Technology. Since 2008, two of her projects have been funded (EU Structural Funds, the Republic of Cyprus and the Research Promotion Organization). These projects are entitled 'Physical activity, nutritional habits and self-regulation as factors of health and development – an example Cyprus and Egypt' and 'The development of self-regulation skills in nurses in the clinical setting'.*

Dr Kalavana has presented her work as a speaker at international professional conferences such as the Annual European Health Psychology Society Conference, the International Congress of Psychology and the European Congress of Psychology. She has published her research in scientific journals such as the Journal of Health Psychology, *the* International Journal of Public Health, Appetite, *the* Medical Health Science Journal *and* Educational Psychology in Practice.

Monitoring time can be considered as one of the basic functions of human development which was vital in the evolution of human cognitive functioning.[1] Researchers Ricci Bitti and Rossi argued that the notion of time is something we experience and manipulate in our daily life, and which enables us to build our identity.[2] Low expectations for the future, or an orientation toward the present, can be considered as contributors of high-risk behaviours.

Since Pause Button Therapy (PBT) aims to alter individuals' time perspective, and to teach the individuals to consider themselves in future possible situations by facilitating prospective memory and the formation of implementation intentions, it is thus essential to present in this chapter the theoretical background of time perspective research that this therapy relies on, justifying why PBT is gaining such considerable attention as a procedure that facilitates behaviour change.

The Notion of Time[3]

One of the biggest challenges in human life is time estimation. In the 17th century Descartes regarded time perception as something very subjective and innate – that is, that time was perceived by each individual differently – 'I interpret time the way I want, not as it is.' The Copernican-Newtonian revolution turned time into a real, measurable object, arguing that time is not a perception of the inside man. The philosopher Kant was the first to mention that the notion of time may have a psychological aspect. Pierre Janet viewed time within two dimensions: man adapts himself to time; and he creates it.[4] Fraisse established three levels of human reaction in terms of time – physiological time, time past/perception of time, and speculation of time – and in this way introduced the concept of time within the spectrum of cognitive and motivational factors.[5] Lewin also addressed the impact of time perspective on psychological conditions, arguing that time perspective is part of the individual's orientation of psychological past and future existing at a given time.[6] Nuttin pointed out that time perspective is facilitated by working out cognitively our needs, intentions and projects.[7]

Furthermore, he underlines the importance of future and past events on present behaviour, further indicating the impact of future. At the same time, Albert Bandura's self-efficacy theory argues that generated self-efficacy beliefs which influence behavioural self-regulation are shaped based on the tripartite of past experiences, current appraisals, and reflections on future selections.[8]

In addition, Reale's research has presented that the notion of past and future, more than anything else, is gradually internalized as personal experience, and thus ego allows the individual to delay gratification.[9]

Finally, contemporary psychology outlined the study of psychological time in general, and the time perspective in particular, and thus Zimbardo and colleagues have proposed a broad conceptualization of temporal perspective as a foundational process in both individual and societal functioning level.[10] Specifically, temporal perspective is assumed to be a non-conscious process in which temporal factors contribute to a leading connective role in the relationship between personal and social experiences, and thus give meaning and order to life events.

In order to encode, store and recall experienced events, or even for the purpose of forming expectations, goals and imaginative views, temporal cognitive frames are used. Further, concrete representation of the present is based somewhere between abstract psychological constructions of prior past and anticipated future events. Therefore, current decision making in the immediate life space, and the delay of several sources of gratification, can lead to undesirable consequences and is probably based on reconstructing the past and constructing the future.

Time Perspective

A number of terms in psychology, such as 'consideration of future consequences', 'delay gratification' and 'impulsivity', underline the importance of future outcomes in the 'here and now' decisions.[11] Many behaviours, and especially health-related behaviours, include conditions in which there is a need for a decision based on immediate pleasure and potential future benefits.[12] Therefore, a decision that needs to be taken regarding behaviour requires the value to be set on the potential positive outcomes at some point in the future.

Time perspective is said to yield a strong impact on individuals' judgements, decisions and actions.[13] Future time perspective has been conceptualized as 'the present anticipation of future goals',[14] deriving from motivational goal-setting and including different temporal distance of future goals. For instance, a short temporal distance can be the goal of not eating chocolates tomorrow, and a long temporal distance goal can be the avoidance of everyday consumption of chocolates in order to lose 15 kg in the following six months. Future time perspective has been generally described as a conceptualization in terms of time for a particular life domain. Husman defined future time perspective as an instrument that facilitates goal achievement in the future.[15]

According to time perspective theory our view of ourselves, our world, and our relationships is filtered through temporally cognitive processes.[16] Thus, we learn to distinguish our personal experiences into the temporal categories of past, present and future. 'Present-oriented' individuals tend to rely on the immediate, salient aspects of the stimulus when making decisions and taking actions, whereas 'Future-oriented' individuals' decisions are based on anticipated consequences of imagined future scenarios. The third category, 'Past-oriented', refers to individuals who tend to rely on recall of reconstructed scenarios. Finally, many studies have presented that being future-oriented is associated with several optimal outcomes.

Zimbardo and Boyd visualized time perspective as a situational element that is cognitive in nature.[17] Time perspective is considered as a global perspective on the future and the present. Present has also been distinguished into present *hedonistic* and present *fatalistic* perspectives.

Hedonistic people are locked in the present because they are only seeking immediate satisfaction and hedonic pleasures (e.g. addictions, TV, partying, sex, etc.). However, Zimbardo and Boyd argued that people under the hedonistic category are not happy and they often feel depressed.[18] Fatalistic people, Seligman argued, experience no control over future events and thus feel depressed and unmotivated to engage in any sort of activity.[19]

Furthermore, Zimbardo and Boyd argued that achievement, goal-setting, risk-taking and other behaviours have their basis in time perspective constructs.[20] Regarding this notion, Nurmi viewed future time orientation within the terms of basic processes of motivation, planning and evaluation.[21] *Motivation* refers to people's interests for the future, *planning* refers to how people plan the implementation of these interests, and *evaluation* refers to the extent that people expect their interests to be implemented.

Lens regarded time perspective as a cognitive-motivational concept.[22] A concept that is figured by 'extension' and 'valence'. 'Extension' shows the degree of remoteness of the representation in time. The 'valence' of the future time perspective presents the value ascribed to a life domain in the future. The way a person appreciates a certain life domain in the future has an important role in defining the concept of future time perspective as a motivational factor.

Moreover, Peetsma perceived that the concept of time perspective is aimed at a certain life domain in terms of three components: 'cognition', 'affect', and 'behavioural intention'.[23] 'Cognition' includes ideas or expectations with regard to the future and the awareness of the surrounded reality. 'Affect' involves feelings or general affect towards a particular life domain in the future. 'Behavioural intention' refers to the targeted future behaviour that needs to be adopted or changed. Therefore, time perspective focuses on the degree to which individuals value a goal or life domain in the present or in the future, their intention to implement this goal, and their feelings and emotions towards this goal or life domain.

Time Perspective and Changing Behaviour

Given the complexity of time perspective, several researchers attempted to relate future orientation or present orientation to their effects on selected outcome behaviours. Therefore, future orientation has been related to many positive consequences for individuals in Western society, such as higher socio-economic status, superior academic achievement, less sensation-seeking, and fewer health-risk behaviours.

In contrast, individuals with dominant present orientation have been associated with many negative life consequences, such as mental health problems, juvenile delinquency, crime, addictions.[24]

Furthermore, a study on time perspective and the activation of our idealistic (what we would like to be) versus pragmatic (right now) selves argued (a) that distal rather than proximal time perspective enhances the preference for identity over instrumental benefits; (b) individuals construe themselves as relatively more idealistic than pragmatic when primed with a distal rather than proximal time perspective and (c) self-activation mediates the effect of time perspective on preferences.[25] In other words, time perspective influences our two opposite poles – our idealistic selves (defined as the mental representation that considers principles and values above any practical considerations) and our pragmatic selves (characterized as an action-oriented mental representation which is mostly guided by practical concerns) and their reactions such as in mundane and critical decision-making.

In addition to the above research on the time perspective's influence on the two opposite poles of the self, another study on the individual differences in time perspective and the auto-noetic experience (the human capacity for remembering) showed that future and present-hedonistic orientations exerted separate influences on auto-noetic experiences, whereas past orientations exerted no influence on auto-noetic experience.[26] Therefore, being more future-oriented and being more present-hedonistic-oriented predicted more vivid auto-noetic (self-knowing) experiences during both remembering and episodic future thinking.

Moreover, time perspective, especially in schools and professional careers, has been considered as one of the strong predictors of students' learning behaviour and academic achievement.[27] Specifically, in a study regarding future time perspective in three aspects of life such as school and professional careers, social relations and leisure time, it was found that future time perspective influenced the development of academic achievement through the growth of investment in learning. Moreover, the study showed the positive effects of the long-term time perspective in school, professional career and social relationships.[28]

Thus, time dimension is important for learning motivation since it incorporates steps that have implications for the future.[29] For instance, Bembenutty and Karabenick perceived time perspective within a self-regulated framework, arguing that future time perspective is a component of students' toolkits for learning to complete academic tasks over time.[30]

Therefore, based on the above research studies regarding time perspective, there are no doubts whatsoever of the importance of time perspective on cognitive ability, consciousness, decision-making and human actions.

The Relation between Time Perspective, Health-related Behaviours and Health-related Protective Behaviours

Health behaviours are the most important tools for the prevention and management of cardiovascular and metabolic diseases. Recent indications encourage people to quit smoking, maintain a healthy body weight, engage in daily physical activity and reduce their intake of saturated and trans fats, cholesterol, sodium and simple sugars. One of the major factors predicting the willingness of people to commit to these kinds of health-promoting behaviours is time perspective. Time perspective and future discounting has been associated with individuals' decision-making.[31] Further, a related concept of time preference involves the extent to which people favour immediate utility over delayed utility, and how value is assigned to future and present events. For instance, the long-term benefits of much health-promoting behaviour are discounted to different degrees because of the implications for present behaviour. For instance, avoidance of cardiovascular disease can be translated into a long-term low-fat diet, but fatty foods taste good!

Health-related risk behaviours (e.g. smoking, excessive use of alcohol) are considered as actions that may result in immediate or long-term negative health consequences, whereas health-related protective behaviours (e.g. condom use, healthy eating, physical exercise) are actions that maintain or improve health status. Many theories that attempted to explain and to facilitate risk-reduction and health-promotion focused only on the aspects of providing information and incomplete explanations of how behaviour changes. Theories that recognized the role of motivational aspects of behaviours offered a better explanation for why people adopt a health-related protective behaviour.[32] One of the constructs of motivation that has been recognized as one of the very promising factors in predicting health-related risk and protective behaviours is time perspective.

Existing theoretical models of health behaviour include variables such as the cost and perceived benefits of a healthy behaviour, supporting the notion that valuing the future determines health-promoting behaviours. Furthermore, some of the many existing studies have reported a strong relationship between time perspective and several behaviours, e.g. the use of substances, condom use/safer sexual practices, fruit and vegetable intake and physical activity.[33]

Specifically, in health-related research it was shown that present time perspective was positively related to risky driving, and also associated with frequent sexual behaviour and a greater number of sexual partners.[34] Additionally, Wills, Sandy, and Yaeger and Keough, Zimbardo and Boyd found a positive relation between present time perspective and substance use.[35] On the other hand, research showed that individuals with stronger future time perspective tend to report fewer risk behaviours such as risky driving,[36] delayed onset of sexual activity with fewer sexual partners,[37] and less substance use.[38] Furthermore, it is also found that future time perspective is positively related to health protective behaviours such as condom use, exercise and healthy eating behaviour.[39]

Furthermore, delay discounting and time perspective were found to significantly improve the incremental prediction of tobacco, alcohol, drug use, exercise frequency, eating breakfast, wearing a safety belt, estimated longevity and health concerns.[40] Also, a recent study on adolescents' expectations regarding their future, predicted health behaviours in early adulthood.[41] More specifically, the study showed that adolescents who rated their chances of attending college or university exercised more frequently and smoked fewer cigarettes in young adulthood.

Pause Button Therapy and Time Perspective

As it is presented above, time perspective has been considered as one of the most important aspects in predicting decision-making and action. Achievement, goal-setting and risk-taking have been considered as having their basis in time perspective. Pause Button Therapy was developed based on time perspective theories in order to encourage individuals to develop a broader understanding of their actions, and to develop a more future-oriented perspective regarding healthy actions. Future orientation, of course, involves processes such as motivation, planning and evaluation.

PBT uses the idea of the Pause, Rewind, Fast Forward and Play buttons on remote control devices to help people give themselves more thinking time when faced with decisions. By making the best possible use of that time to weigh up the potential consequences of their actions, this allows them to explore the value of a present and a future action and to practise, or strengthen, their ability to develop a more future-oriented perspective and to strengthen further delaying gratification.

PBT encourages the auto-noetic consciousness to take action and stop automaticity of reactions. PBT teaches people how to develop significant self-regulation skills such as goal-setting, planning, self-monitoring, emotional control and coping with present problems that occur while working towards a goal. PBT is probably the only tool in existence right now that bridges the gap between behavioural intention and actual behaviour, and this is what classifies it as an effective therapeutic procedure that can lead to successful behavioural change!

In their book, *The Time Paradox*, Zimbardo and Boyd address the realization that changes of behaviour are less likely to happen when – as is often the case – seminars on 'behavioural change' are led by future-thinkers attempting to change the ways of present-thinking people, or even those with issues resulting from their past still hovering in the background of their day-to-day lives.[42]

They argue that if emphasis were put on understanding the importance of an individual's time bias, that person could then be trained to see how their thinking could improve if they switched from being stuck in the past/present to using more of a future-based decision-making process.

We would suggest this is not a million miles from what has been put together in Pause Button Therapy. Without going into Fast Forward to consider how your actions will impact on your future, you may simply take what you have seen as the obviously easier route, with no thought for tomorrow, or five minutes' time from now, or next year, or how those same time slots will be for your family or friends.

Pressing Pause gives you that safe zone, without the pressure of the moment, to go into the future on Fast Forward to look, feel, hear, smell, really understand what might be the outcome of your 'now' choice. To alter your relationship with time, just for a few moments. Then, over a period of weeks, if used and re-used, you will find your Pause Button is actually giving you a critical understanding of how all your actions, choices, thoughts – pretty much most aspects of your day-to-day life – will be more positive if you think ahead that bit more.

Giving you, as we've said so many times, an easier way of life *in the present.*

RESEARCH AND TRAINING OPPORTUNITIES

Martin and Gay ask the education community: 'Would you like to be more involved?'

We are very keen to continue to gain research evidence of the effectiveness of the PBT methodology across a range of settings. All staff attending training courses are provided with materials to record progress and evidence changes in perception and behaviour. Additional copies can be downloaded from the Teacher Resource Page on our website, and we are in discussions around how to collect data via web-based systems. We are developing an app for both the iPhone and Android markets that will enable us to collect data of PBT in use.

We would like to develop more partnerships with Higher Education providers who may be interested in incorporating PBT into coursework for teachers, educational psychologists or other professionals who work face to face with children or families. Gay Jones has already run an introductory PBT course for postgraduate psychology students at the University of Cyprus. We hope that action research modules could be developed. These would support participants in utilizing real-life situations and questions within a coursework context. This valuable research will also contribute to the growing body of evidence for PBT as a flexible and effective tool for change.

We can be contacted at welcome@pbtherapy.com

Training for Therapists

If you are interested in gaining accreditation to use Pause Button Therapy as a stand-alone therapy tool, please contact us for details.

All listed Pause Button Therapists are qualified and have undertaken additional training to ensure consistent, high-quality interventions. They are registered members of the International Pause Button Therapists Association (IPBTA).

Training for Parents and Carers

Bespoke training for parents and carers to support the use of PBT is available. Half-day training can be delivered on-site to groups.

In addition, Pause Button Therapy International provides training and support for employees, practitioners, youth offending teams, health professionals, local authorities, Primary Care Trusts and GP consortia, along with web-based resources and forums for both users and practitioners.

Training for Teachers and Education Professionals

In addition to providing training courses for the education sector, we provide a Teacher Resource Centre.

Those undertaking the PBT training for use with children and young people are expected to acquire understanding of the development, aims and theory of PBT, plus:

- be able to identify situations where PBT might be used to support change
- be able to effectively use PBT across the curriculum
- have developed a set of clear best practice guidelines for the setting
- have accessed resources and ideas for extending the use of PBT in school- or setting-based activities
- feel confident in implementing the technique immediately
- know how to access web-based support, ideas and additional resources
- be able to evaluate impact, and collect evidence and design programmes to achieve effective outcomes
- be able to analyze perceptions and outcomes relating to those undertaking PBT

A training course for staff is available for groups of 20 or more participants.

Contact details: www.pausebuttontherapy.com

FURTHER RESOURCES

Books

The Beck Diet Solution, Judith Beck
Organizational Transitions: Managing Complex Change, Beckhard and Harris (Addison-Wesley Series on Organization Development), 1987
Stop Thinking, Start Living, Richard Carlson
Overcoming Addiction, Bob Conklin
Hope with Eating Disorders, Lynn Crilly (Hay House, 2012)
When You Choose Your Actions You Are Choosing the Consequences, Gary Fenton (Characterpath.com, 2008)
Train Your Emotions – Dealing with Anger, Lloyd Irvin (www.articlesbase.com)
The Alternative to Cause and Effect: Behaviors Occur by Constraint and Response, excerpts from *Changing Your Stripes*, Matt Moody PhD
Staying Well with Guided Imagery, Belleruth Naparstek
Life Between Death and Rebirth: Sixteen Lectures by Rudolf Steiner, Rudolf Steiner (SteinerBooks Inc., 1975)

Websites

http://www.beckdietsolution.com/

REFERENCES

Chapter 2
A Closer Look at PBT in Use

1. A. Smellie, Mail Online

2. http://www.dailymail.co.uk/health/article-2035900/Tattoo-removal-Like-Megan-Fox-beginning-regret-inkings.html

3. http://www.bodyjewelleryshop.com/body_piercing_information/location_types/

4. thefreedictionary.com, The American Heritage® Dictionary of the English Language (4th edn), Collins English Dictionary – Complete and Unabridged, Collins Thesaurus of the English Language, WordNet 3.0, Farlex clipart collection. © 2003-2011 Princeton University, Farlex Inc.

Chapter 3
PBT in Your Hands

1. http://www.msassociation.org/publications/winter08/cover.story.asp

2. http://www.pravsworld.com/content/inspiration/283/think-before-you-act

3. L. Irvin, *Train Your Emotions – Dealing with Anger*, http://www.articlesbase.com/martial-arts-articles/train-your-emotions-dealing-with-anger-1076012.html

4. R. Carlson, PhD, *Stop Thinking, Start Living* (Element, 2003)

Chapter 4
The Inevitability of Karma

1. R. Steiner, *Life Between Death and Rebirth: Sixteen Lectures by Rudolf Steiner* (SteinerBooks Inc., 1975)

2. M. Moody, PhD, The Alternative to Cause and Effect: Behaviors Occur by Constraint and Response, from Changing Your Stripes: http://www.calldrmatt.com/Cause&Effect.htm

3. http://phys.org/news140173735.html

4. The Zimbardo Time Perspective Inventory (ZTPI); http://psych.stanford.edu/cgi-bin/remark3/rws3.pl?FORM=psych187_ztpi

5. Beckhard and Harris, *Organizational Transitions: Managing Complex Change* (Addison-Wesley Series on Organization Development, 1987)

6. G. Fenton, When you choose your actions you are choosing the consequences (Characterpath.com, 2008): http://www.characterpath.com/blog/?p=30

7. www.merriam-webster.com/dictionary

8. Ibid.

9. S. R. Covey, The 7 Habits of Highly Effective People (Simon & Schuster, 2004)

10. http://en.wikipedia.org/wiki/Butterfly_effect

Chapter 6
21 Days to Change Your Life

1. U. Dimberg, M. Thunberg and K. Elmehed, 'Unconscious Facial Reactions to Emotional Facial Expressions', *Psychological Science* 11 (2000): 86

2. R. Stefoff, *Charles Darwin and the Evolution Revolution*

(Oxford University Press, 1996); http://bjsm.bmj.com/
content/40/10/822.full

3. 'Good Dingo – an article on the behavior of the once
    domesticated Dingo', *Natural History Magazine*; http://www.
    naturalhistorymag.com/samplings/101906/good-dingo

4. S. Webb, *The Effects of Repetition on Vocabulary Knowledge*
    (Oxford University Press Abstract, 2007)

5. D. Crundall, B. Andrews, E. van Loon and P. Chapman,
    'Commentary training improves responsiveness to hazards in a
    driving simulator', Accident Research Unit, School of Psychology,
    University of Nottingham, March 2009

6. Received 13 March, 2009

7. www.enneagraminstitute.com

8. www.en.wikipedia.org/wiki/Four_stages_of_competence

9. J. McCrone, *Readings: How to Create a Habit* (Dichotomistic,
    2006)

Chapter 7
How Do You Use the Remote?

1. http://en.wikipedia.org/wiki/Remote_control

2. 'Logitech Study Shows Multiple Remote Controls Hindering
    Entertainment Experiences Around the Globe', http://www.
    logitech.com/en-us/172/7748

3. http://en.wikipedia.org/wiki/The_Heist_(Derren_Brown_special)

Chapter 8
Changing Your Mind

1. http://en.wikipedia.org/wiki/List_of_thought_processes

2. R. Carlson, PhD, *Stop Thinking, Start Living* (Element, 2003)

3. http://www.alcoholics-anonymous.org.uk/bigbook/pdf/
   BigBook_chapt5.pdf

4. http://theopalproject.com/types.html

5. http://www.ocdsymptoms.co.uk/symptoms-category.html

6. http://www.anxietycoach.com/causes-panic-attacks.html

7. http://www.shopliftingprevention.org/TheIssue/
   TheActOfShoplifting.htm

8. S. J. Bedwell, 'Four Ways to Shorten Your Grocery Store Trip',
   January 2012 www.self.com

9. http://www.womenshealth.gov/publications/our-publications/
   fact-sheet/bulimia-nervosa.cfm

Chapter 9
How PBT Could Help Cut Government Spending

1. R. Camber, 'Criminals let out on bail responsible for one fifth
   of burglaries', *Mail* Online: http://www.dailymail.co.uk/news/
   article-2028624

2. http://www.victimsupport.org.uk

3. *National Offender Management Service Annual Report and
   Accounts* 2010-11: http://www.justice.gov.uk/downloads/
   statistics/hmps/prison-costs-summary-10-11.pdf

4. Y. C. Wang, K. McPherson, T. Marsh *et al.*, 'Health and economic
   burden of the projected obesity trends in the USA and the UK',
   Lancet 378 (2011): 815-25

5. D. Batty, 'Antidepressant use in England soars', *The Guardian*, December 2011

6. J. Hope, 'Doctors want patient time doubled', *Mail* Online: http://www.dailymail.co.uk/health/article-57944

7. E. L. Lim, K. G. Hollingsworth, B. S. Aribisala, M. J. Chen, J. C. Mathers and R. Taylor, 'Reversal of type 2 diabetes: normalisation of beta cell function in association with decreased pancreas and liver triacylglycerol', *Diabetologia* DOI 10.1007/s00125-011-2204-7

8. http://www.bury.nhs.uk/news-and-media-centre/press-releases/2010/11112010.aspx

9. http://news.bbc.co.uk/2/hi/health/2710717.stm

10. http://www.eatingdisorders411.com/medical-complications.html

11. National cost-impact report: Implementing the NICE clinical guideline on obsessive-compulsive disorder. Issue date: December 2005

12. Statistics on Smoking: England, 2011, NHS Information Centre

13. http://www.dailymail.co.uk/health/article-1304433

Chapter 10
Using PBT with Children and Young People

1. G. Bateson, *2000 Steps to an Ecology of Mind* (University of Chicago Press, 1973): 457-59

2. Harvard neurologist and expert on epilepsy Frances Jensen, alarmed at her own teens' behaviour, found that neuroscientists are discovering teenagers' nerve cells are sluggish when it comes to connecting the frontal lobe with the rest of the brain. They have less of a fatty coating called myelin – which is needed for nerve signals to communicate quickly. And the frontal lobe is the part of the brain that looks at consequences, so it seems

young people's ability to judge what's a good idea and what's not is simply 'incomplete wiring'

3. Charles Desforges and Alberto Abouchaar, 'The Impact of Parental Involvement, Parental Support and Family Education on Pupil Achievements and Adjustment: A Literature Review', 2003; http://bgfl.org/bgfl/custom/files_uploaded/uploaded_resources/18617/Desforges.pdf

4. 1st Report of the House of Commons Education Committee, Behaviour and Discipline in Schools 26/01/11 (Point 22)

Chapter 11
Rioting, Bullying: Children and Their Feedback

1. http://www.guardian.co.uk/uk/2011/aug/31/youngest-london-rioter-boy-11-sentenced

2. http://www.dailymail.co.uk/news/article-2027064

3. http://www.dailymail.co.uk/news/article-2038323

4. http://www.bbc.co.uk/news/uk-england-london-15923875

5. J. R. Goldstein, 'A Secular Trend toward Earlier Male Sexual Maturity: Evidence from Shifting Ages of Male Young Adult Mortality', www.plosone.org/article/info%3Adoi%2F10.1371%2Fjournal.pone.0014826

6. J. Insely, 'Car insurance: satellite boxes "make young drivers safer"', The Guardian, April 2012

Chapter 12
Putting Your 'Sensible Head' On

1. http://en.wikipedia.org/wiki/Worzel_Gummidge

2. American Heritage® Dictionary of the English Language (4th edn)

3. http://www.dailymail.co.uk/news/article-1318638

4. D. Miller, 'Council binmen banned from crossing the ROAD due to 'elf and safety fears they could get run over', *Mail* Online

5. P. Zimbardo and J. Boyd, *The Time Paradox: The New Psychology of Time that Will Change Your Life* (New York: Free Press, 2008)

6. http://jobmob.co.il/blog/funniest-resume-mistakes

7. G. Kaufman, 'Why do stars make bad choices?', MTV.com

Appendix
Future-thinking and PBT: An Academic Perspective

1. T. Suddendorf and M. C. Corballis, *Mental Time Travel and the Evolution of Human Mind* (New York: Basic Books, 1997)

2. P. E. Ricci Bitti and V. Rossi, *Vivere et Progettare di Tempo* (Milan: Franco Angeli, 1988)

3. M. D'Alessio, A. Guarino, V. De Pascalis and P. G. Zimbardo, 'Testing Zimbardo's Stanford Time Perspective Inventory (STPI)', 2003; P. G. Zimbardo, *Strategies for Coping with Social Traps: Time Perspectives Influences.* Paper presented at the 98th Annual Convention of American Psychological Association, Boston, August; http://www.zimbardo.com/downloads/2003%20Art%20Time%20and%20Society.pdf

4. P. Janet, *L'évolution de la Mémoire et de la Notion du Temps* (Paris: Chanine, 1928)

5. P. Fraisse, *Psychologie du Temps* (Paris: PUF, 1957)

6. K. Lewin, *Field Theory in the Social Sciences: Selected Theoretical Papers* (New York: Harper, 1951)

7. J. R. Nuttin, *Future Time Perspective and Motivation: Theory and Research Method* (Hillsdale, NJ: Erlbaum, 1985)

8. A. Bandura, *Self-efficacy: The Exercise of Control* (New York: Freeman, 1997)

9. P. Reale, *Ricerche Sperimentali sulla Nozione di Tempo* (Bologna: Patron, 1984)

10. P. G. Zimbardo and J. N. Boyd, 'Putting Time in Perspective: a valid, reliable individual-differences metric', *Journal of Personality and Social Psychology* 77 (1999): 1271-88; P. G. Zimbardo, K. A. Keough and J. N. Boyd, 'Present time perspective as a predictor of risky driving', *Personality and Individual Differences* 23 (1997): 1007-1023

11. A. Strathman, F. Gleicher, D. Boninger and C. Edwards, 'The consideration of future consequences: Weighing immediate and distant outcomes of behavior', *Journal of Personality and Social Psychology* 66 (1994): 742-52; M. Cuskelly, M. Einam and A. Jobling, 'Delay gratification in young adults with Down syndrome', *Down Syndrome Research and Practice* 7 (2001): 60-67; T. Allen, G. Moeller, H. Rhoades and D. Cherek, 'Impulsivity and history of drug dependence', *Drug and Alcohol Dependence* 50 (1998): 137-45

12. B. Piko, A. Luszczynska, E. Gibbons and M. Tekozel, 'A culture-based study of personal and social influences of adolescent smoking', *European Journal of Public Health* 15 (2005): 393-98

13. J. Nuttin and W. Lens, *Future Time Perspective and Motivation: Theory and Research Method* (Leuven: Leuven University Press, 1985); P. G. Zimbardo and J. N. Boyd, 'Putting time in perspective: a valid, reliable individual-differences metric', *Journal of Personality and Social Psychology* 77 (1999): 1271-88

14. J. Husman and W. Lens, 'The role of the future in student motivation', *Educational Psychologist* 34 (1999): 113-25

15. J. Husman, *The effect of perceptions of the future on intrinsic motivation* (unpublished doctoral dissertation. Austin, Texas: University of Texas, 1998)

16. A. Gonsalez and P. G. Zimbardo, 'Time in Perspective', *Psychology Today* 19 (1985): 21-26; P. G. Zimbardo, K. A. Keough and J. N. Boyd, 'Present time perspective as a predictor of risky driving', *Personality and Individual Differences* 23 (1997): 1007-1023

17. P. G. Zimbardo and J. N. Boyd, 'Putting time in perspective: a valid, reliable individual-differences metric', *Journal of Personality and Social Psychology* 77 (1999): 1271-88

18. Ibid.

19. M. E. P. Seligman, *Helplessness: On Depression, Development, and Death* (San Francisco: Freeman, 1975)

20. P. G. Zimbardo and J. N. Boyd, 'Putting time in perspective: a valid, reliable individual-differences metric', *Journal of Personality and Social Psychology* 77 (1999): 1271-88

21. J. E. Nurmi, 'Planning, motivation, and evaluation in orientation to the future: a latent structure analysis', *Scandinavian Journal of Psychology* 30 (1989): 64-71

22. W. Lens, 'Future time perspective: a cognitive-motivation concept', in D. R. Brown and J. Veroff (eds), *Frontiers of Motivational Psychology* (New York: Springer Lens, 1986): 173-90

23. T. T. D. Peetsma, *Measurement of Dutch Secondary Students' Perspectives Concerning their Future* (Amsterdam: Universiteit van Amsterdam, 1985); T. T. D. Peetsma, 'Future time perspective as a predictor of school investment', *Scandinavian Journal of Educational Research* 44 (2000): 177-92

24. M. L. De Volder and W. Lens, 'Academic achievement and future time perspective as a cognitive-motivational concept', *Journal of Personality and Social Psychology* 42 (1982): 566-71; R. Levine, *A Geography of Time: The Temporal Misadventure of a Social Psychologist, or How Every Culture Keeps Time Just a Little Bit Differently* (New York: Basic Books, 1997); J. Nuttin, *Future Time Perspective and Motivation: Theory and Research Method* (Hillsdale, NJ: Erlbaum, 1985); A. Strathman,

F. Gleicher, D. Boninger and C. Edwards, 'The consideration of future consequences: Weighing immediate and distant outcomes of behavior', *Journal of Personality and Social Psychology* 66 (1994): 742-52; Z. Zaleski, *Psychology of Future Orientation* (Lublin: Towarzystwo Naukowe KUL, 1994)

25. Y. Kivetz and T. R. Tyler, 'Tomorrow I'll be me: The effect of time perspective on the activation of idealistic versus pragmatic selves', *Organizational Behavior and Human Decision Processes* 102 (2007): 193-211

26. K. M. Arnold, K. B. McDermott and K. K. Szpunar, 'Individual differences in time perspective predict autonoetic experience', *Consciousness and Cognition* 20 (2011): 712-19

27. J. Husman and W. Lens, 'The role of the future in student motivation', *Educational Psychologists* 34 (1999): 113-25; W. Lens, J. Simons and S. Dewitte, 'Student motivation and self-regulation as a function of future time perspective and perceived instrumentality', in S. Volet and S. Jarvela (eds), *Motivation in Learning Contexts: Theoretical Advances and Methodological Implications* (New York: Pergamon, 2001): 233-48

28. T. T. D. Peetsma and I. Van der Veen, 'Relations between the development of future time perspective in three life domains, investment in learning, and academic achievement', *Learning and Instruction* 21 (2011): 481-94

29. J. O. Raynor and E. E. Entin, 'The function of future orientation as a determinant of human behavior in step-path theory of action', *International Journal of Psychology* 18 (1983): 463-87

30. H. Bembenutty and S. A. Karabenick, 'Inherent association between academic delay gratification, future time perspective, and self-regulated learning', *Educational Psychology Review* 16.1 (2004): 35-57

31. L. C. Guthrie, S. C. Butler and M. M. Ward, 'Time perspective and socioeconomic status: a link to socioeconomic disparities in health?', *Social Science and Medicine* 68.12 (2009): 2145-51

32. J. D. Fisher and W. A. Fisher, 'Changing AIDS-risk behavior', *Psychological Bulletin* 111 (1992): 455-474; J. O. Prochaska, C. C. Di Clemente and J. C. Norcross, 'In search of how people change. Applications to addictive behavior', *American Psychologist* 47 (1992): 1102-1114

33. K. Kirby and N. Petry, 'Heroin and cocaine abusers have higher discount rates for delayed rewards than alcoholics or non-drug-using controls', *Society for the Study of Addiction* 99 (2004): 461-471; B. Reynolds, J. Richards, K. Horn and K. Karraker, 'Delay discounting and probability discounting as related to cigarette smoking status in adults', *Behavioural Processes* 65 (2004): 35-42; C. Agnew and T. Loving, 'Future time orientation and condom use: Attitudes, intentions, and behavior', *Journal of Social Behavior and Personality* 13 (1998): 755-64; J. Hamilton, K. Kives, V. Micevski and S. Grace, 'Time perspective and health promoting behavior in a cardiac rehabilitation population', *Behavioral Medicine* 28 (2003): 132-39

34. P. G. Zimbardo, K. A. Keough and J. N. Boyd, 'Present time perspective as a predictor of risky driving', *Personality and Individual Differences* 23 (1997): 1007-1023; S. Rothspan and S. J. Read, 'Present versus future time perspective and HIV risk among heterosexual college students', *Health Psychology* 15 (1996):131-43

35. T. A. Wills, J. M. Sandy and A. M. Yeager, 'Time perspective and early onset substance use: A model based on stress-coping theory', *Psychology Addictive Behaviors* 15 (2001): 118-25; K. A. Keough, P. G. Zimbardo and J. N. Boyd, 'Who's smoking, drinking, and using drugs? Time perspective as a predictor of substance use', *Basic and Applied Social Psychology* 21.2 (1999): 149-64

36. P. G. Zimbardo, K. A. Keough and J. N. Boyd, 'Present time perspective as a predictor of risky driving', *Personality and Individual Differences* 23 (1997): 1007-1023

37. S. Rothspan and S. J. Read, 'Present versus future time perspective and HIV risk among heterosexual college students', *Health Psychology* 15 (1996):131-43

38. T. A. Wills, J. M. Sandy and A. M. Yeager, 'Time perspective and early onset substance use: A model based on stress-coping theory', *Psychology Addictive Behaviors* 15 (2001): 118-25

39. C. Dilorio, M. Parsons, S. Lehr, D. Adame and J. Carlone, 'Factors associated with use of safer sex practices among college freshmen', *Research in Nursing and Health* 16 (1993): 343-350; N. Mahon, T. Yarcheski and A. Yarcheski, 'Future time perspective and positive health practices in young adults: An extension', *Perceptual and Motor Skills* 84 (1997): 1299-1304

40. J. R. Daugherty and G. L. Brase, 'Taking time to be healthy: Predicting health behaviour with delay discounting and time perspective', *Personality and Individual Differences* 48 (2010): 202-207

41. T. W. McDade, L. Chyu, G. J. Duncan, L. T. Hoyt, L. D. Doane and E. K. Adam, 'Adolescents' expectations for the future predict health behaviors in early adulthood', *Social Science and Medicine* 73 (2011): 391-98

42. P. Zimbardo and J. Boyd, *The Time Paradox: The New Psychology of Time that Will Change Your Life* (New York: Free Press, 2008)

INDEX

Page references in *italic* indicate displayed quotations of people not otherwise mentioned on the page. The acronym PBT is used for Pause Button Therapy.

NOTES

NOTES

THE GASTRIC MIND BAND

Martin and Marion Shirran
with Fiona Graham

The idea of using the subconscious, rather than invasive gastric band surgery, to convince people they can eat no more than a fraction of their stomach's normal capacity – a Gastric *mind* Band® – caught the public's imagination.

The book of the therapy mixes CBT (Cognitive Behavioural Therapy), NLP (Neuro-Linguistic Programming) and hypnotherapy – in the form of self-hypnosis – to ensure readers approach changing their relationship with food rather than adopting a short-term 'diet'-type situation. It includes an introduction to PBT.

The reader is taken on a detailed journey through building up a picture of why they're overweight, understanding what their body needs, portion control, looking at the ways we fool ourselves into eating when we shouldn't be – and how to overcome it – and finally, how to use the subconscious to believe there is a band restricting the stomach's capacity.

Published by Hay House in January 2013.

JOIN THE HAY HOUSE FAMILY

As the leading self-help, mind, body and spirit publisher in the UK, we'd like to welcome you to our family so that you can enjoy all the benefits our website has to offer.

 **EXTRACTS** from a selection of your favourite author titles

 COMPETITIONS, PRIZES & SPECIAL OFFERS Win extracts, money off, downloads and so much more

 **LISTEN** to a range of radio interviews and our latest audio publications

 CELEBRATE YOUR BIRTHDAY An inspiring gift will be sent your way

 **LATEST NEWS** Keep up with the latest news from and about our authors

 ATTEND OUR AUTHOR EVENTS Be the first to hear about our author events

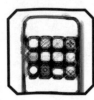 **iPHONE APPS** Download your favourite app for your iPhone

 HAY HOUSE INFORMATION Ask us anything, all enquiries answered

join us online at **www.hayhouse.co.uk**

 292B Kensal Road, London W10 5BE
T: 020 8962 1230 E: info@hayhouse.co.uk

ABOUT THE AUTHORS

Martin Shirran, a former PR and marketing director, met **Marion** on a hypnotherapy course when she was a disenchanted language teacher frustrated at dealing with disinterested and unmotivated youngsters.

Intrigued by psychology since taking a course on sales and marketing, Martin undertook a REBT course at Birmingham University presented by renowned lecturer Professor Windy Dryden. Martin has also undertaken courses in NLP. The couple set up the Elite Clinics in Spain in 2004, and are certified and registered with the American Board and British Institutes of Hypnotherapy. Their GmB (Gastric Mind Band) weight-loss therapy is now widely emulated; Martin says imitation is the sincerest form of flattery!

They read psychology books widely, though Martin defines his theoretical knowledge as less significant than the life experiences of being married, divorced, burying close family members and travelling the world.

Marion, who gained an Honours degree from Lancaster University, has a nurse, doctor and midwife in the family, but is 'far too squeamish to do anything involving blood and guts'. Working in therapy seemed perfect for her!

Martin holds a UK private pilot's licence and an RYA Offshore Yacht Master's Licence. Marion's main pastime is cooking Thai, Chinese and Indian food alongside contemporary classics.

Fiona Graham, formerly a UK journalist, has worked on the Shirrans' books for a number of years.

www.pausebuttontherapy.com